THE SHORELINE OF WONDER

Dear Carol,
Thank you for
being here and for
your love of the
Sun
Love,
Austin

CREATIVITY**MATTERS!**

C**M!**

BERKELEY, CALFORNIA

THE SHORELINE OF WONDER

ON BEING CREATIVE

AUSTIN HILL SHAW

Published in the United States by CREATIVITY**MATTERS!**
Berkeley, California

ISBN: 978-0-9854800-1-1

First Edition: 2012

To Epiphany, Sierra Lucia, and Lorenzo Delmar

And in loving memory of

Mathew Baxter

Elizabeth Binyon Smith

Ely Clarkson Shaw

and

Ron Takaki

Admiration for creativity is universal,
so creativity must be part of the hidden reserves
of all of us.

—*David Richo*

TABLE OF CONTENTS

INTRODUCTION:
THE GROUND AND THE PATH OF CREATIVITY

Tell me, what is it you plan to do with
your one wild and precious life?
—Mary Oliver

On July 4, 1998, I found myself on a small ledge in Yosemite Valley, most of the way up an 800-foot pillar of rock known as the Rostrum. I had just finished climbing a difficult section, secured myself to an anchor, and began belaying my climbing partner. Because of a curve in the route, I was unable to see him as he climbed up the crack system below. So I kept a light tug on the rope, pulled in the slack as he ascended, and took in the sweeping view.

It was late afternoon. The sun was low and illuminating the west-facing formations in front of me. On the South Rim, Bridalveil Falls—a 600-foot, free-falling waterfall—was framed by the Cathedral formations and the Leaning Tower. To the north, the West Face of El Capitan commanded the view. Far below on the valley floor, the Ponderosa and Lodgepole pines looked more like blades of grass. The sky was blue, vast, and devoid of clouds.

After a short time, I noticed a change in the coloring of Bridalveil Falls. Normally a lacey white, it was now brownish-red. At first, I thought it might be sediment washed down from a distant rainstorm in the southern Yosemite high country. But the color was *too* red, and I hadn't seen a rain cloud in the area for days.

As I continued staring at the waterfall, the color morphed again, this time towards red-orange. Then orange. Then yellow-orange. Then yellow. I realized what was happening. The sun descending in the west, the invisible vapor surrounding the waterfall, and my position on the side of the cliff were all aligned in such a way that I was witnessing a display of the spectrum of visible light, one color after another. From the tail end of the infrared to the invisible beginnings of ultraviolet, the infinite colors of the rainbow were presenting themselves to me one micro-shade at a time.

My heart pounded in my chest. I yelled to my partner to look toward the falls. But he was deep in the awkward crack, using arm bars and knee locks to inch his way upwards, and unable to see it.

Anchored to the wall, I stood there transfixed as the waterfall continued to move through the greens, blues, and violets. In less than ten minutes it was over. The waterfall looked as it had before— a white veil of turbulence unraveling in the dry summer air.

I contemplated what had just happened as my partner climbed up to the ledge. Out of an ordinary day, a prism of sorts had arisen out of nowhere. The clear mountain sunshine which illuminated the valley had been split into parts by the vapor surrounding the waterfall. And like the view you might imagine walking widthwise across a rainbow, the individual colors weren't experienced all at once, but one after another—the way music unfolds over time.

My mind began to race around all the factors involved to cause such a thing. I thought of the heat and pressure under the earth that had created the granite pillar I stood upon and the force of the glaciers that widened the valley long ago. I envisioned the unique triangular shape of the water molecule and its ability to refract light. I recalled the years spent training to climb such a route and the great fortune that I was looking at the waterfall and not down at my partner at that moment. I contemplated my eyes' ability to perceive form and color. I thought of the waterfall a mile in front of me and the sun some 90 million miles behind me. So many factors had contributed to my experience. So little of what was "my experience" was actually my own.

These thoughts spawned others. I thought of the incredible efforts of the Egyptians and Mesoamericans and those who built Stonehenge to arrange enormous stones to track the movements of heavenly bodies. I remembered my excitement as an 11-year-old boy at the movies, watching Indiana Jones locate the Arch of the Covenant by placing a jewel atop a staff in a shaft of light. Like the water launching into the void, an intricate web of interrelated images cascaded through my mind, accompanied by feelings of reverence, gratitude, and a giddy irony: There I was on Independence Day feeling an exhilarating sense of *interdependence* and a profound sense of *wholeness.*

From Lodgepole Pines to granite monoliths, from hand-carved furniture to designer couches, from stellar jays to human beings, from odds on the upcoming ballgame to emerging theories of evolution, from objects in nature and artifacts of humanity—nothing is static. Nothing exists in isolation. And the experience, the true, heartfelt experience of all of these things can never be adequately described in words. I realize now that what I glimpsed on that day from the ledge on the cliff was the foundation of creativity: the luminous dynamism, miraculous interplay, and mysterious complexity that produce the world we experience.

In Search of Genuine Creativity

What is genuine creativity and how might we embrace it as a way of life?

Through my own experiences as a writer, artist, and architectural designer, through innumerable conversations with others, and by studying the writings of people throughout history and from all over the world, including the abundant research of contemporary psychologists, neurologists and other scientists, I have been exploring these questions for most of my adult life. From my exploration two trends have emerged.

In the first trend, creativity occupies the highest level of human development and is dependent upon other, more basic needs, to be satisfied before it can be actuated. Psychologist Abraham Maslow, for example, placed creativity at the apex of his now famous *Hierarchy of Needs*, at the level of *self-actualization*. Maslow suggested that only when the needs of the lower four levels—physiological, safety, love/belonging, and esteem—had been fulfilled that creativity, along with spontaneity, morality, and lack of prejudice, was even possible.

These words are paralleled at the collective level by statesman John Adams, who suggested that for there to be any act we deem "creative," a hard-fought stabilization must be in place. In 1780, during the tumultuous infancy of the United States, Adams, in a letter to his wife, Abigail, wrote, "I must study politics and war that my sons may have liberty to study mathematics and philosophy. My sons ought to study mathematics and philosophy, geography, natural history, naval architecture, navigation, commerce and agriculture in order to give their children a right to study painting, poetry, music, architecture, statuary, tapestry, and porcelain."

However, once this stabilization is in place, Lynne C. Levesque, author of *Breakthrough Creativity,* says that creativity lies in the personal growth of individuals: "To be creative you have to contribute something different from what you've done before. Your results need not be original to the world; few results truly meet that criterion. In fact, most results are built on the work of others." Levesque here seems to build a bridge between acknowledging the interdependent aspect of creativity and the importance of the individual paying attention to his or her own personal growth.

The second trend suggests that creativity is always already available. Psychologist George Kneller, for example, suggested that creativity stems from appreciation and is available by simply viewing our ordinary world in a new way. He writes, "To think creatively, we must be able to look afresh at what we normally take for granted." Author and Jewish mystic Etty Hillesum thought that we needn't produce anything in order to be creative; simply the way one works with one's self is enough: "I do believe it is possible to create, even without ever writing a word or painting a picture, by simply molding one's inner life. And that, too, is a deed." Even Abraham Maslow, in a different vein, lamented, "The key question isn't 'What fosters creativity?' But it is why in God's name isn't everyone creative? Where was the human potential lost? How was it crippled? I think therefore a good question might be not why do people create? But why do people not create or innovate? We have got to abandon that sense of amazement in the face of creativity, as if it were a miracle if anybody created anything."

In this second trend, the crux seems to be in the *allowing.* How do we, as George Kneller suggested, "look afresh" at the world, as though we could just change out our eyeballs for new ones? How do we, in the world of Etty Hillesum, "mold our inner life" as though it were as accessible as a wet piece of clay?

Adding to the challenge, Albert Einstein once said, "The most beautiful thing we can experience is the mysterious. It is the [creative] source of all true art and all science. He to whom this emotion is a stranger, who can no longer pause to wonder and stand rapt in awe, is as good as dead: his eyes are closed." But given Einstein's criteria, for many of us, for much of the time, [we have to admit:] we *are* as good as dead. Pausing without doing anything seems like a waste of time, especially if we have deadlines looming over our heads. And standing in rapt awe? Have we not filled our heads with facts and information to avoid such primitive gestures?

If we take both trends to be true, if we begin to see creativity as *both* the highest expression of human development *and* as something that is always already available, new possibilities arise. From the view that creativity is always available, we recognize the possibility of experiencing the vibrancy of the world that surrounds us *as the basis of our lives* and not some exotic exception. From the first trend, in order to celebrate to our fullest extent the agility of the human body, the rare and precious plasticity of the human brain, as well as the boundless expanse of the human spirit, we also recognize that we can *exert ourselves* to bring the experience of creativity into all aspects of our lives.

Together, these two trends form 1) the recognition of a basic ground that supports us, a ground that is inherently creative in nature and 2) a path that helps us to deepen our intimacy with that creative ground while enriching our own lives and the lives of others through our willingness to traverse it.

Deep inside we know this to be true: When we find ourselves moved by the world around us, we feel inspired no matter what we are doing. In this way, brushing our teeth can be as much of a creative act as is designing a building façade, writing a score of music, or contemplating the chemical sequence for producing a new material. Every act has the potential to be *experienced* as a creative act because they all involve the arising of a whole new world from the one of the previous moment. Likewise, we can take those inspiring experiences and *actively create*, rolling up our sleeves, stepping beyond the edges of our comfort zones, and working to develop what's inspiring to us into something that can be shared with others.

The Ground and the Path of Creativity

Creativity, then, has two fundamental aspects: the **Ground of Creativity** and the **Path of Creativity**. The **Ground of Creativity** describes my experience from the ledge in Yosemite Valley, an experience imbued with the qualities of luminous dynamism, miraculous interplay, and mysterious complexity. Even though we may be in the habit of experiencing our lives as a series of isolated, disjointed events separated by time and space, taking a step back and widening our view reveals a very different picture: Everything is changing, everything is interrelated, and try as we might, we will never figure it all out—mystery and uncertainty are inherent to the experience of being human. In the words of John Muir, who petitioned for the protection of Yosemite and other places like it, "When we try to pick out anything by itself, we find it hitched to everything else in the universe." The Ground of Creativity manifests in an infinite variety of ways. Look how it swirls around you! Listen to the signature laugh of a long-dead grandfather bellowing from the throat of his three-year-old granddaughter. Look at the ebb and flow of the tides as they respond to the persistent tugs of the sun and the moon. Feel the connection in a façade of Doric columns fronting a new bank in Omaha, Nebraska to an ancient culture two millennia and eight time zones away. The things you experience here and now have their origins in the there and then. The golden threads of this moment will reweave the universe of the future.

What unites all these different experiences are not the individual characteristics of the players, where they take place, the thoughts they may kindle, or the feelings they may evoke. What unites them all is the Ground of Creativity—the vast and intricate interplay of causes and conditions that makes each one of them possible.

Furthermore, the Ground of Creativity is whole; there is no sense of excess or lack, or of good or bad. Everything is complete within itself. Everything is simply *as it is*. A waterfall, for example, that is spectrumming through the colors of the rainbow is just as whole and complete as one that is not, or even one that has dried up for the season. We may *prefer* one experience of the waterfall over the other; we may prefer the roaring spring runoff to the trickle of late fall. But each variation of the waterfall is perfectly whole. It is only our opinions and expectations that make one waterfall more desirable than another.

The ordinary events that take place in your life—waking up in the morning, taking a shower, listening to the news, envisioning the day before you—are all based on extraordinary contingencies, extraordinary webs of connectedness spanning outward in all directions. None of them unfolds as a series of isolated events separated in time and space. They unfold as the intimate and unceasing reconfiguring of wholeness, always changing, always interconnected, and always perfectly complete.

The Ground of Creativity isn't the "ground" because it is solid or particularly stable, but because it supports the arisings of the world you experience with its enduring interrelatedness and ever-present wholeness, external arisings such as clear summer days and climbing gear and internal arisings such as feelings of exhilaration and thoughts of fear and reverence alike.

The Ground of Creativity supports you and the giving of your creative gifts. Before you do anything, the Ground of Creativity is there. While you create, the Ground of Creativity is there. When you finish creating, the Ground of Creativity is there. When what you finished creating dissolves in time, the Ground of Creativity is there. While the individual players, actions, and settings are constantly changing, what does not change is their dynamism, interdependence, and mysterious, immeasurable wholeness. The Ground of Creativity describes the very foundations of the creative universe we inhabit: A universe that is always changing, always intimately connected, always mysteriously complex, and always whole.

The second fundamental aspect of creativity describes your ability to engage all this. This is the **Path of Creativity**. This is where the infinite play of the creative universe intersects your finite sense of who you are as an individual.

On that summer's day in 1998, for example, the Path of Creativity describes the totality of the environment—towering rocks and turbulent water, brilliant sunlight and still, dry air, and the huge sense of scale and space that comes from a glacial valley like Yosemite—meeting my internal experience as a climber and the shared experience with my climbing partner.

For us, rock climbing and rock craft was an art, aligning our physical strength and flexibility with our mental focus to explore bold and beautiful natural areas. We climbed as a celebration of our tiny selves using knobs, crystals, and crack systems to ascend huge vertical faces hundreds of times our size. We cherished the ephemeral nature of our own lives playing themselves out upon million-year-old rock formations. We loved the concentration and effort, the knowledge of knots, anchors, and gear placement, the language of safety and the management of risk, the calming of fear through breath and visualization, and the yelps and yodels of terror and ecstasy alike. We climbed—as with any genuine creative undertaking—to feel our small selves merge with the Ground of Creativity, the luminous dynamism, miraculous interplay, and mysterious complexity of the world around us. Seeing the spectrum of color from the belay ledge high above the valley floor was just another expression of that: the unification of heaven and earth, the cosmic fire of the sun passing through the life-giving qualities of water, revealing in the spectrum the infinite colors of the creative universe.

If the Ground of Creativity is the unceasing reconfiguration of wholeness moment after moment, the Path of Creativity describes our lifelong journey of learning to more skillfully engage that sense of wholeness in everything we do. Or stated a bit differently, the Path of Creativity describes our commitment to embracing the universal appeal of creativity as a way of life.

The Path of Creativity is the marriage of our two fundamental ways of relating with the world around us: **being** and **doing**. Being allows the Ground of Creativity to engage and transform us. Doing allows us to engage and transform it. The play of the universe requires both.

Being allows for the **experience of insight**, which I'll explore in depth in Part II. Insight marks portions of the creative process when something unbeknown to us makes itself known. Being generates hunches, intuitions, seed ideas and concepts, or makes new relationships between existing ideas or concepts. When we are able to simply *be*, the ungraspable becomes graspable. Being allows the external sensorial world to penetrate us. Being also allows our inward thoughts and emotions to move through us without our trying to hold onto them or pushing them aside. Instead, like a horse put out to pasture, we allow our thoughts and emotions to either settle and rest or to gallop about free and unrestrained. In other words like a canyon or a flute, we allow things to flow through us.

Being can have a number of qualities. It can involve rising above the appearance of things being isolated and experiencing instead the interrelationship of the parts to the whole, like the experience you have of landscape when you are flying over it in an airplane. Or like snaking along the ground, being can also be the experience of immersing oneself in the sights, smells, sounds, and textures of the environments around you. A third way of being combines the first two. It involves the ability to experience the panoramic view, the interrelationship of the parts to the whole, while simultaneous dropping into the full-body experience of the environments around us. Like a rainbow containing all the colors, this is the fullest expression of being, the full spectrum of awareness across our bodies, minds, and spirits contained in a singular experience. Regardless, when we are able to simply be, there is a sense of creative insight *coming to us*. We feel alive and nourished, even when we're doing nothing at all.

By relaxing into whatever is happening while it is happening, we send out an open and unconditioned invitation to the world. More specifically, by relaxing our self-imposed boundaries, we simultane-ous build the lightning rods and aqueducts that invite the creative universe to fill us up.

When **doing,** we act upon our insights and elaborate them through measurable means. This active part of the creative process is what I call **manifestation,** which we'll also explore in depth later on. When doing, concepts are formed, sketches are made, deliberate movements guide our bodies, glimpses of the ungraspable are put into words, and words into sentences that can be shared with others. Doing takes the ineffable experience of fully being and roots it in the realm of discrete ideas, actions, and form.

In this way, creatively doing can also take a number of basic forms. It can involve descending or grounding, taking what has been experienced on the mountain top and converting it into actual form, like taking an experience of universal love and translating it into a single poem or a program to serve at-risk youth. It can involve integrating that full-body sensorial experience into a discrete path of action, like the one who becomes a chef or an advocate for local foods after a momentous bite of fresh trout served in a white wine sauce. And doing can mirror the fullest expression of being, unify-ing *both* panoramic awareness *and* deep sensorial awareness and translating *that* into fully embodied actions, actions that reverber-ate outward like thunder due to our full-person alignment. Like a dancer both expressing and transcending the melody, cadence, and emotion of the music, or a chemist experiencing a sudden empathic understanding of a compound that allows her to work with it in an unforeseen way, this third sort of doing describes the coveted experience of creative flow, a sort of doing that is so powerful that ordinary time and space seem to dissolve.

Creative doing is neither blind nor habitual. It is not like a set of unalterable marching orders issued by a dictator to be carried out no matter what. Doing maintains a connection to both the ungraspable nature of initial insights as well as to the new insights that reveal themselves as a creative process unfolds in time. In other words, as you act—as you participate in the reordering of wholeness—you keep one hand raised toward the heavens and the other on the pen gliding across your sketch pad.

Together being and doing are like a full cycle of breath. First, with our lungs completely empty, we breathe the world in. By allowing ourselves to *relax* and receive, we feel nourished and inspired. Then, like a weightlifter exhaling as he hoists a heavy load, we breathe it back out as we *effort* to do something meaningful; we breathe out and actively participate in the reconfiguration of wholeness.

All of which leads us to my definition of creativity.[1] In its most basic expression, The Path of Creativity is simply 1) connecting with the world and 2) affecting the world in a meaningful way. Connecting with the world, being with it just as it is, produces the experience of insight. Affecting the world in a meaningful way, doing something to share our insights with others, is the process of manifestation.

There is a third aspect of creativity which involves the ability to be and to do *simultaneously*, to profoundly connect with the world around us while affecting it *at the same time*. This third aspect I call **Self-expression**, which we'll also explore in depth later on. For now, however, it is important that we first develop our understanding of simply the being and doing of creativity, of insight and manifestation respectively.

---

[1] For those interested, I go into depth on the origins of my definition of creativity in my last book, *Between the Bridge and the Water: Death, Rebirth, and Creative Awakening.*

Please notice that my definition of creativity has nothing to do with novelty or uniqueness. Though novelty and uniqueness are often associated with more conventional definitions of creativity, such qualities need not be sought after. They need not be sought after because they are already deeply embedded in both the continuous unfolding of the universe and our relationship to it. With the Ground of Creativity as the backdrop to *everything*, the universe is always new; it is always morphing into something different from the moment before. And since each and every one of us experiences that morphing through our own unrepeatable lens upon the world, and since that lens is constantly changing, too, our perspective is always unique.

As an individual, you are experiencing your own, very personal *version* of the world around you. Your experience reflects and reciprocates the connection and wholeness that is the Ground of Creativity. And it is unique; no one will ever experience the world in quite the same way as you. Because it is unique, your perspective and your gifts to the universe are unfathomably rare and precious. Your existence—your astonishing ability to think, feel, and act—is also the play of the universe. You, too, are the result of an infinite number of causes and conditions. You, too, participate in shaping the universe and contribute to its arisings in the future.

Despite this ongoing, intimate connection to the Ground of Creativity, your life can feel, much of the time, like your own little world. Are you surrounded by people who love and appreciate you, but still feel lonely? Do you feel detached from the places you inhabit? Do you feel a sense of separation between you and your experiences? Do you feel frustrated that you seem unable to engage the world in a positive or meaningful way? Within your unique experience of the world there are grand opportunities and great challenges alike. The opportunities come from your receptivity to the Ground of Creativity, from your felt sense of interdependence and wholeness. Your challenges arise when you ignore, deny, or fail to access this ground, or when you find yourself pulling away, which leads to feelings of isolation and loss.

The Path of Creativity, then, describes your moment-to-moment experience of reestablishing your felt sense of change, interdependence, and intrigue with the world around you, your felt sense of actively participating in the ceaseless unfolding of creation. By contrast, you stray from the path when you fall into a myopic, self-centered stance that holds the world at a distance. While the Ground of Creativity is *always* at play in the unfolding of your experience, the Path of Creativity describes your ability to engage the ground more and more intimately. With increased intimacy comes increased awareness: The more you are able to engage the Ground of Creativity, the more you gain perspective on the motivations *behind* the choices you make.

Ultimately, it is up to you to decide how you walk the path. You and you alone can walk it. No one else can walk it for you. If you walk the path with courage and openness, your life intersects the vital and luminous Ground of Creativity. You resonate with the dynamic life force of all things, animate and inanimate alike. If you walk the path carelessly or with a closed heart, you isolate yourself. You disconnect from the Ground of Creativity and the underlying vibrancy of the universe that pervades you.

The Journey Ahead

The Shoreline of Wonder is a guide to understand, explore, and activate two fundamental aspects of creativity—the Ground and the Path—in your own *experience of living*. Since the Ground of Creativity is happening all the time, the first section will help you to *notice* how it occurs, then to *experience* it in the various aspects of your life. Part I, "The Ground of Creativity," will unveil the Ground of Creativity as it occurs in the world and as it occurs in *you*.

With a felt sense of the Ground of Creativity established, the next three chapters in Part II—"Cultivating Insight," "Manifestation," and "Self-expression"—will address the Path of Creativity. The chapters are both sequential and cumulative. Each one builds upon the others. The first chapter, "Cultivating Insight," will explore the mysterious world of creative inspiration, helping us move from a sense of being creatively blocked or isolated to a sense of feeling profoundly connected. The second chapter, "Manifestation," will explore the ins and outs of giving form to our creative insights, emphasizing our inherent connectedness and dependence upon all that surrounds us. In the third chapter, "Self-expression," the path culminates with the luminous awareness and unceasing inspiration that arises by fully claiming our creative powers and learning to both relax and actively engage the world *simultaneously*. Self-expression, when fully developed, is none other than learning to access the creative life force in everything we do.

Along the way, we'll enter into the lives of some remarkably creative individuals. We'll explore the mystical experience of a scientist that led him to uncover one of the fundamental laws of nature. We'll follow the outrageous ambition and rigorous planning of an artist couple to realize their seminal work. And we'll look at the outer and inner life of the preeminent scholar on world religions and uncover the secrets leading to a genuinely creative life.

The final section of this book, "Fruition," will tie everything together, but with two, very different approaches. In "Putting It All Together" I will focus upon the external aspects of creativity, recounting my journey as part of a team working to develop a new building at a health and wellness center in Baja, Mexico. "Putting It All Together" will also illustrate how the various components of the Path of Creativity correspond to the domains of science, art, and religion. In "Pulling It All Apart" I will explore the equally important internal journey of embracing a genuinely creative life, the sometimes joyous, sometimes painful aspects of confronting one's self-defeating behaviors in order to rise up to a creative challenge or, in my case, the burning and claustrophobia I had to endure in my own maturation as a creator, the challenge, growth, and learning that came from finding myself in the midst of a seemingly impossible, seemingly irreconcilable situation.

There are many excellent books out there on creativity that have been instrumental in shaping my own understanding of the subject.[2] This book focuses on helping you to recognize the boundless display of creativity that is happening all the time and to harness it as your experience toward leading a deeply enriching life. Our drive to create—to paint landscapes, to plan parties, to savor colors, and solve problems—gets to the very core of what it means to be human. All of us are natural creators. And, in our heart of hearts, all of us

---

[2] If you are as fascinated by the creative process as much as I am, I encourage you visit the resource section of my website www.austinhillshaw.com for my own, ever-growing list of inspiration.

THE SHORELINE OF WONDER

wish to connect with the world and to affect it in a meaningful way. As such, this book should be less like learning a foreign language and more like flipping through a family album. Because your ability to create is already part of who you are, my hope is that you experience these ideas as somehow *familiar*.

Still, no matter what you may learn about the creative process from this or other sources, unless you internalize that learning—unless you integrate such knowledge into your own experience—it doesn't do you much good in the long run. If the words on these pages resonate with you, please take the time to see how they fit into your own life. Make them personal. I will be pleased if you are inspired by these words. I will be overjoyed, however, if you take these ideas and make them a part of your own creative process.[3]

Like any creative undertaking, these words in front of you have arisen from an inconceivable line of causes and conditions, including the efforts of many others, who, like myself, have chosen to explore the creative process through their own unique lens on the world. To all of these people, known and unknown, and the people and situations that shaped their expansive understandings of the world, I am eternally grateful and wholly indebted. In order to keep the chapters simple and powerful, the specific influences I drew upon can be found at the back of the book. If some chapter or topic is of particular interest to you, I encourage you to explore it further. This can benefit your lifelong journey of deepening your heartfelt relationship to both the Ground and Path of Creativity.

It is time, now, to begin. Acknowledge any doubts or excitement you may have. Feel into the texture of this moment and just let it

---

[3] The ideas contained in this book will be soon followed by an accompanying workbook, *Further Along the Shoreline of Wonder: How to Live a Creative Life.*

be. Relax. It is time, now, to rest in the self-existing nature of your present experience. It is time, now, to feel into your intimate connectedness with everything around you. It is time, now, to settle into the fundamental wholeness and deep and profound mystery that is always already available.

It is time, *now*, to connect with the Ground of Creativity.

PART ONE

THE GROUND OF CREATIVITY

THE BIG BANG, BEGINNINGLESS TIME, AND THE JOURNEY OF THE CREATIVE UNIVERSE

If you wish to make an apple pie from scratch,
you must first create the universe.
—Carl Sagan

It's all in there, waiting, just waiting in the time before time, the universe, *our universe,* packed unimaginably tight, indistinguishably tight, packed into a single point, a point infinitely smaller than a grain of sand, the rawest of raw materials awaiting the miraculous complexity of a single atom, all the solids, liquids, and gasses that will come from those atoms, the stuff of the stars, planets, and moons, indeed entire galaxies and clusters of galaxies, the cosmic winds, the lines that will become horizons and the edges of door frames, the planes that will become meadows and the surfaces of alpine lakes, and the volumes that will become oceans and mountains and bathtubs full of splish-splashy toddlers, the light that will erupt in the east each morning and flood through the kitchen window, the future debates over what to call Pluto, the weight of autumn and the promise of spring, Orion's Belt and Cassiopeia, up and down, near and far, left and right, the carbon atom, the water molecule, semiconductors, bacteria and viruses, fish and flowering plants, the early nervous system, indeed conscious self-awareness itself—the awareness of being aware—packed in there, too, packed in there with memory and with language and with all those sparklers of emotions—love, grief, and anger rubbing shoulders with the asteroids and the dark matter, the possibilities of Jesus, Buddha, Mohammad, Lao Tzu cohabitating in dimensionless space, the cave paintings of Lascaux, the Pyramids of Giza, the sculptures of Bernini, the paintings of Kandinsky, the soulful jazz improvisations of Miles Davis, polio and the vaccine for polio, waterfalls spectrumming through the colors of the rainbow, moonlight on the mountains, and the unrepeatable configuration that is you, all this floating in that awesome sea of nothingness, packed, simply *PACKED*, waiting, just waiting like an unlit match on a shrine box, waiting like the bedrock in a fault zone, waiting like a landmine in a jungle, feeling in its own strange way the feeling of being so intensely small, hot, and dense, having absolutely no way of knowing what it will become and yet becoming *everything*, with no need to reconcile or repress anything, simply waiting for that improbable moment, that nudge, that flick of the wrist, the magic words uttered, and *BOOM!*

The universe as we know it began.

When the 57-year-old Russian-born abstract painter Mark Rothko, was asked how long it takes him to make one of his paintings, he replied, "Fifty-seven years." Rothko, who was known for his long contemplative process of staring at his canvases, punctuated by flurries of activity, captured the fact that the whole of our lives leads to and is contained within any act in the present. Rothko's statement was far more accurate than what most artists probably believe, indeed most people, and still he was off by about 14 billion years, which is the current reigning estimate for the age of our universe.

For creativity to act as a force that deepens our connection with the world in which we live, it is necessary that we have some understanding, or perhaps more importantly, *appreciation* for our universe, a universe where humanity's recent surges of innovation are, as a friend of mine likes to say, but the tiniest of wiggly bits at the far edge of time. Indeed, in our own small neck of the woods, historian John McPhee once said that if you were to represent the entire history of the earth by a man with his arms extended to either side, you could eradicate all of human history with a single swipe of a nail file.

Our planet is part of one solar system among 200–400 billion solar systems in our galaxy, the Milky Way, and the Milky Way is part of an estimated 170 billion galaxies scattered throughout the known universe. There may be no other life out there, or the universe may be full of it. There may be planets in the midst of various stages of evolution, from those where the life has just become visible to the naked eye, to those where they've long figured out how to keep a few parking spaces open in dense urban areas without the threat of meter maids patrolling the streets. As of now, no one can say for certain.

Neither the shortness of our history as a species, nor our tiny, localized sphere of influence, however, makes our lives meaningless or insignificant. Quite the contrary, our lives and all that we do with them are *unspeakably precious*. Even with the weight of the threats of overpopulation, nuclear proliferation, global warming, the poisoning of the biosphere, and the shrugs and groans of the economy, all of our lives and the world in which we live are worthy of *reverence*—not despite these struggles and difficulties, but because of them and because of all of the joys and sorrows of the human drama as well, for they too reflect the play of the universe. For us to be born into all this with a capable physical body, with the capacities for sensation and emotion, with a tireless workhorse of a heart thumping inside our chest, and a subtle and powerful mind that travels backwards and forwards in time, is nothing shy of amazing.

Clearly life is not without its challenges. Indeed the first of the Four Noble Truths of the Buddha was the truth of suffering. We can work diligently all our lives gathering material wealth and resources, we can set up our lives in a way that suits our most refined and elegant tastes. But no matter what we do, we can't avoid suffering. We will fail to get what we believe we deserve, watch things we've worked hard on deteriorate, and lose people we love. What we *can* do is embrace these events as reflections of the unfolding of the universe. The path of genuine creativity, then, is not an avoidance of the wonders and tragedies of life. It fully embraces them.

As individuals, we all have our stories about what we have and have not got. Each and every one of us knows that we have ways of being in the world that are empowering and other ways that trip us up again and again. While a part of us dreams of better ways of doing things, we also waste precious resources, dominate other species, and castigate outsiders we see as threats. And as the days and weeks roll on over the course of our lives, we will play out many narratives, sub-narratives and meta-narratives, many of them regarding our sense of how creative we perceive ourselves to be. Some days our creativity will feel as alive and bountiful as the rainforest. Others it will feel as dry and empty as a salt flat.

In order to better understand our own desire to create—be it savory meals, pen and ink sketches, or wheel-spun pottery—let's take a step back and look at the creative universe that has been at work long before there were any of us around. Let's take a step back and look at what was going on in the overwhelming majority of time that preceded the human drama. Let's look at a creative universe that has given rise to a solar system with a watery planet, and a planet that has given rise to life, and life that has given rise to conscious self-awareness. Let's get into the three qualities that make up the Ground of Creativity. Let's drop into the experience of the luminous dynamism, miraculous interplay, and mysterious complexity that is the canvas upon which the events of our lives unfold.

In doing so, we will begin the process of understanding what we can do to surrender our limiting beliefs about who we are as individuals and, instead, allow for the possibility of connection, expansion, and creativity in everything we do.

Like a director carefully examining a venue so as to craft his plan for the space, the success of our creative endeavors begins with a clear understanding of the way things are. Such an exploration can also help us to expose and debunk certain myths surrounding our own, uniquely human way of creating, common myths that when we unknowingly subscribe to them hinder our natural ability as creators. Such myths include 1) the belief that creativity is an aptitude of certain gifted individuals and not others 2) the idea that the capacity to create is held in the individual, and 3) the concept that creativity is inherent to some activities, such as art and music, but not to others, such as science and engineering.

As we explore the creative universe it is helpful that we see it for what it is: An epic tale intimately tied to our own ability to create, an epic tale that continues to unfold *right now*. As we explore the creative universe, let us allow that epic tale to debunk those myths that hinder our natural ability to create.

Luminous Dynamism

Since the very beginning, if indeed there was a beginning, the universe has been dynamic and ever-changing. It has been in a ceaseless process of forming, morphing, destroying, and recreating itself anew over and over again, long before we humans were on the scene. This is the universe that, over the course of 10 billion years (as far as we know it), has given rise to life, and in the last several hundred thousand years (or somewhere thereabouts), has given rise to conscious self-awareness. And, like any great creation, it didn't happen all at once, but over incredibly long periods of time, punctuated by fabulous cycles of creativity and destruction, of becoming, abiding, and ceasing, of birth and death, of gradual stabilization and all hell breaking loose.

The universe isn't static, it's dynamic. Quarks flip this way and that. Electrons blaze around protons. Moons race around planets, planets race around the centers of their solar systems, the solar systems race around the centers of their galaxies, the galaxies race around other galaxies, all forming fabulous spiraling patterns and corkscrews as they move unceasingly through absolute space. The universe continues to expand outward with the force of the original, primordial birth scream. And each of these celestial objects spins on its own axis, wobbling like Sufi dancers, forming hourglass shapes with their movements. Light itself runs unencumbered across the vast expanses of empty space. From the tiniest known substances dancing in their clouds of probability up to the largest galactic clusters, the universe is in constant motion.

Nor does the universe behave like a Good Samaritan, crossing the street only where it is supposed to, respecting people's property, refraining from spitting on the sidewalk. No, it jay walks, loiters, and runs into the street without thinking. The dynamic universe explodes and implodes, flings its material outward like rice at a wedding reception, then, caught by the force of gravity, gathers it back together like a miser gobbling up his neighbors' resources. Comets slam into planets, meteors scrape across the upper edges of the atmosphere, entire galaxies colonize smaller galaxies, ripping those stars and solar systems apart, reworking them into strange and wonderful forms. When stars run out of fuel, some of them pull to the side of the road and go dim, others blow up, while still others implode with such force that they bend the space-time continuum like a cosmic funhouse mirror. Van Gogh's skies weren't portraits of insanity; they were raw, honest depictions of a swirling, blazing, dynamic universe.

If we look closely, we see that the universe we inhabit has been in unceasing play between two main types of change, those leading to increased order and complexity and those leading to disarray, dissolution, and chaos. In the same way each new line we write in a journal brings the ink in the pen a few drops closer to its end, it is important that we honor both of these forces for both are needed to keep our creativity vital.

According to current scientific theory, the universe began with a bang, an explosion of inconceivable force that initiated the expansion of the universe outward from a single point. As the universe expanded, it also cooled from a temperature that well exceeded the melting point of all known objects to a temperature that allowed matter to begin to congeal. The heat and density was so intense that the four main known forces acting in our universe—gravity, electrostatic, and the strong and weak nuclear forces—were indistinguishable. Everything was one. In other words, the universe began as pure energy, something that was too hot and too dense to accommodate matter, or anything else, as we know it today.

Think of a time in your own life when you felt the underlying unity of all things, an experience that would, in time, lead you to take a whole new course of action in your life. At that moment all you felt was the pure energy of experience. Perhaps you just fell in love. Perhaps you awoke for the first time after a car accident. As we will see later on, the conditions that precede genuine insight look a lot like the origins of the universe: A vibrant, unfettered, indescribable aliveness awaiting a still unknown formation.

As the energy was able to disperse, it allowed for something new, for that pure energy to reconfigure itself into the basic building blocks of the material world, first the subatomic particles, and from that, the first atoms.

Feel the significance of that moment: Out of this inconceivably hot, densely packed cosmic plasma there came a time when the conditions were finally favorable for a positively charged proton to capture in its orbit a negatively charged electron. The first atoms, primarily hydrogen and helium, were born, creating a whole new universe with unforeseen opportunities for further changes.

This atomic universe was a curious beast. In comparison to the chaos of the plasma universe, it was far more organized. And it grew colder and darker with each passing moment.

Imagine the quality of the universe at that time, still expanding rapidly, full of newly formed hydrogen and helium atoms, and totally dark, prompting cosmologists to call this time "The Cosmic Dark Ages." Perhaps in your own creative pursuits you've experienced such a time, groping along in the darkness, unsure of what to do next. Such times are also part of the creative process and even though they can be uncomfortable, they sometimes lead to amazing things. As a friend of mine once told me on the eve of the fall equinox, "Growth happens in the light, transformation in the darkness."

As the universe expanded further, irregularities in the density of those first atoms, like lumps in a mattress, began to be felt. While the outward expansion of the universe continued (as it does to this day), there was enough room for another force to begin to rear its head in earnest, gravity. It was gravity that pulled these first atoms into amorphous clouds of material, known as nebula. Within the nebula, the hydrogen further began to organize into smaller, denser clouds, and finally into compact spheres. When enough material coalesced and the pressure reached a critical point, the nuclei of hydrogen atoms fused, forming helium and releasing an immense amount of energy. The spheres of gas ignited. The first stars were born.

Like gravity, some aspects of creativity pull things toward one another so that new things, sometimes predictable, sometimes unforeseen, can arise. Like waves upon the ocean and the cycling of the seasons, the creative universe moves through endless cycles of arising, abiding, and ceasing.

Embracing luminous dynamism is essential to our own abilities as humans to create. When we see our lives as static or somehow fixed, or imagine that we were born a certain way and have no ability to change or explore new directions, we cut ourselves off from our natural creativity. Furthermore, when we embrace luminous dynamism, we also embrace impermanence, which is creativity's essential companion. For anything to be created, something else must be altered or destroyed. And, as we create, as we connect with the world and affect it in a meaningful way, so too are we transformed in the process, never to exist quite the same way as we did just a moment before. Finally, the fact that everything is constantly changing means none of us is ever really stuck. Luminous dynamism gives rise to luminous insights, allowing us to experience the world in a whole new light than we did just the moment before, allowing us to experience our lives as endlessly fascinating and unceasingly creative.

In the presence of luminous dynamism the first myth of creativity dissolves: Creativity is not an aptitude of certain gifted individuals. It is a way of *being*, a way of being available to everyone.

MIRACULOUS INTERPLAY

Miraculous interplay is not some extraordinary exception to the creative process; it is the very fabric of the creative process itself. Architect Frank Gehry's masterpiece, the dancing, curving titanium-clad Guggenheim museum in Bilbao, for example, resulted from a combination of the architect's love of sculptural art, a new 3D scanning software that enabled the replication of hand-sculpted mockups, the national pride of the Basque people willing to undertake the project, and a precipitous drop in the cost of titanium from the fall of the Soviet Union. Likewise, the smelting of tin and copper during early human civilization ushered in a new wave of innovation in art, weaponry, and domestic uses that came to be known as the Bronze Age. In men's tennis, the lightweight, carbon-fiber rackets that emerged in the 1980s led to a game of giant serves instead of one of playful rallies.

But there was a time in the universe when titanium, tin, copper, and carbon were non-existent. They too, as well as all of the building blocks of matter, had to be created.

During the Cosmic Dark Ages—the time between when the first atoms were created (200,000–400,000 years after the Big Bang) until the first stars were born (100 million–250 million years after the Big Bang)—the palette of available materials was limited, severely limited. There were no such things as water, or ashes, or dust. There was no light and, therefore, no color.

Only three types of atoms were in existence, hydrogen, helium, and trace amounts of lithium. Hydrogen was also the smallest, lightest, and most versatile of the three, followed by helium, a loner gas that, under normal conditions, likes to keep to itself, and lithium, the universe's first metal. Today, however, we have over 100 elements: Where did the rest of them come from?

Those same early stars were not only the new hearths of light and heat sprinkled throughout the now vastly dark, and increasingly cold, empty space, they became the foundries of matter itself. In the tremendous heat and pressure of the star's center, the smaller atoms were crunched together and fused into heavier ones, the energy released producing the stars' signature heat and light.

All stars convert lighter elements into heavier ones but only some, specifically the large elements, are really prolific in their creativity. Not only are they the foundries of the vast majority of the known elements, they also take care of the distribution. In these larger stars, more than two times the size of our sun, increased gravitational pressure from the extra mass allowed other, heavier elements to be formed. During the star's lifetime, these massive stars would reflect these changes at a grand scale, shrinking by millions of miles as the star would exhaust one fuel type, until enough pressure was built up to fuse the next set of elements. Then, the new, higher energy created at the center would push out, causing the star to expand again, far past its original diameter. The star was kept in a delicate balance, the inward force of gravity balancing the outward force of the energy created at the center with each new type of fuel.

But the biggest creative push of these larger stars occurred at the very end of their lives, with one incredibly violent and prolific moment.

At this point, strangely enough, in the final inhalation of a stellar giant's cataclysmic death, the rest of the elements were created. With all the usable fuel exhausted, these larger stars would collapse under their own weight, then, once a critical point was reached, a point like wrenching the emergency brake while accelerating to the speed of light, the star would explode outward in an instant, forming what is known as a supernova. The force of the explosion itself, the cosmic kickback of all the material compressing to a critical point, then rebounding, produced the needed pressure to fuse all the other elements in an instant. All of which makes supernovas not only the single most destructive events in the universe, but also the brightest known objects and the most creative. Supernovas are the most efficient producers of raw, usable materials, as well as the interstellar delivery service, casting those elements far and wide on the shoulders of behemoth shock waves racing out in all directions. With successive waves of material gathering into clouds, and clouds into spheres, with the rebirth, life, and death of stars, and the flinging of the material back outward into space, the building blocks of the universe began to diversify, populating the vast majority of the periodic chart as we know it today.

Like a strong, sturdy wind carrying seeds to distant places, those new elements with all their own unique and curious properties, would create new possibilities for the universe, new directions in which to go, new eddies to swirl about in, new undertows to contend with. Think of oxygen and its essential importance to our metabolic functioning and its inimitable role in water. Think of phosphorous and its role in coding the chain of DNA. Think of iodine's role in nutrition. Consider the effects of lead pipes in first building, then undermining, the early civilizations. Think of the power of uranium, the heaviest naturally occurring element, and its use in nuclear warheads and its effect on the arms race and geopolitics.

We can see how the continuous change of the universe and the interplay of all of the materials, as well as the forces acting on those materials, have co-created the world that we see today. Without these earlier events, the cycles of birth and destruction, the world that we have today would not have been possible. Without the fusing of hydrogen and helium into other elements over time, and the instantaneous forging of the other elements during supernovas, the elements as we know them would not exist. There would have been no oceans, for without water (two hydrogen and one oxygen) and sodium chloride (one sodium and one chlorine atom) salt water would have been impossible. Nor would there have been land as we know it, for without silicon, the most abundant of the elements in the earth's crust, the land would not be possible. Nor would we have the basic building blocks of life, the incredibly lively and versatile carbon atom, for example, which in its many forms—wood, coal, and petroleum—has also been the primary source of our so-called man-made energy since the age-old invention of fire rings.

Miraculous interplay debunks the second myth of creativity, the idea that the capacity to create is held in the individual. Since the universe has arisen as a continuous process of co-creation, and we have arisen from that universe, our ability to create isn't a reflection of our individuality, but rather of our relatedness to all that surrounds us. None of us exists in isolation. None of us is ever truly alone. Each and every one of us is a product of an inconceivably complex array of causes and conditions extending back in time. Furthermore, in each and every moment, we are affected by a cornucopia of stimuli all around us, including the air that we breathe, the food that we eat, the conversations we have with others, the signs that we read while moving through the city, and the patterns we sense when walking in nature. Our physical bodies may cease at the outermost layers of our skin, but our lives are inextricably linked to the characteristics of our homes and neighborhoods, the trends of our culture, the efficacy of our politics, and the state of the economy.

Miraculous interplay reminds us that all our abilities, including our ability to create, take place within systems, not in isolation.

MYSTERIOUS COMPLEXITY

The qualities of luminous dynamism and miraculous interplay bring us to the third aspect of the creative universe, its mysterious complexity. And when I say mysterious, I mean those aspects of the universe that remain unknowable, those aspects that astound and amaze us, that send chills up and down our spines and launch goose bumps on our skin. Try as we might, they simply don't fit into what our reasoning minds are capable of processing; they defy what can be described in words or numbers alone.

Why is it important to embrace mysterious complexity as one of the key components of the universe in which we live? Throughout the ages, our tendency as human beings has been to try to explain away the unknowns of the universe. On a positive note, our unique and natural desire to know has allowed each and every one of us as individuals, and collectively as a species, to amass an incredibly diverse and prolific understanding of the world, all of which helps us to make informed choices. From the most basic learning, such as the knowledge that fire burns, up to a more nuanced understanding of the tactics used by the credit card salesperson, knowing allows us to maneuver the complexities of the world in which we live and to make sound decisions.

For us to live truly creative lives, however, it is important that we shelve our tendency to apply kneejerk answers to each situation that arises. It is essential that we learn to befriend the groundless, bewildering, deeply mysterious aspects of the universe itself, learning to inhabit those pregnant, amorphous, unborn spaces that mark the origins of any creative process, including the unknowable "space" that gives rise to the universe itself.

There are lots of things out there that make complete sense once you understand the forces that have created them initially and the environments that have shaped them over time. But there are many things that are still shrouded in mystery, because the incredible complexity required for their existence seems to defy what could happen by chance alone. Among these mysteries are 1) the origins of the universe itself 2) the beginning of life on our planet and 3) the beginning of conscious self-awareness, that rare and powerful characteristic that is the single most defining characteristic of us as humans. Let's take a closer look at each of these.

When cosmologists look at the conditions of the present—galaxies that appear to be moving away from us and traces of cosmic radiation in all directions—then roll back the tape, this is what they come up with as the origin of the universe: A pin prick called a singularity— infinitesimally small, hot, and dense—exploded, flinging the universe and the stuff of the universe outward in all directions. This theory, known as the Big Bang, came into vogue in the 1960s and carries its weight to this day.

Still, having exerted genuine effort to fit my fluffy sleeping bag into a space-saving stuff sack during backpacking trips, it's hard for me to imagine compressing it further into a single point, let alone leaving room for the rest of the known universe.

What was this like, in the time before time? Was it like a still, shore-less ocean stretching out in all directions? Was it quiet like a windless night in the dead of winter? Was it a shimmering ball of pure energy with nothing around to shine upon? Was it like that for eons, or more like the brief pause at the end of a long inhalation, the brief pause before the inevitable out breath begins?

And it's not only the singularity that bends my mind but the outward expansion from that single point. What set it in motion? Was it the final implosion of a giant star in a parallel universe that collapsed with such force that it ripped through the fabric of space and time, only to emerge as the universe as we know it? Or was it far stranger, like a practical joke of a cosmic trickster gone fantastically awry?

And what was it expanding into? I've heard it described as a loaf of raisin bread rising in an oven, each raisin representing a galaxy or a cluster of galaxies, each galactic raisin growing farther from its nearest neighbor as the loaf itself expands. Despite the tidy metaphor, I still get tripped up, wondering what the oven might have looked like and who or what was doing the baking.

So I try my luck elsewhere, thinking of other stories involving the origins of the universe, stories that came about before the advent of long-range telescopes and other instruments, stories hashed out around fire circles below blazing starlit skies, stories evolving out of our rare and wonderful curiosity, stories emerging from that insatiable desire to know and to explain.

In the beginning there was... light? Darkness? The Word? Nothing? Everything? Creation myths the world over employ a cast of strange characters, characters with improbable qualities that seem to transcend beginnings or endings, characters with the power to bring order out of formless chaos. Dividers of the tightly bound cosmic eggs, winged serpents, mothers who give birth but who were not born of any, such characters perform a range of acts, from methodically creating the heaven, earth, and all the worldly creatures to cosmic orgasms that birthed the world as we know it in waves of ecstatic shudders.

Creation myths, while often scientifically bogus, become oddly compelling; they pick up the slack where the quantifiable universe falls short. They offer the emotional aspects of our being, and for the inner storyteller in all of us there is a bit of room to maneuver, to cozy up to the inconceivable.

Science does have a word that approximates these unpredictable, unlikely becomings, something called *emergence*, which states that what arises can't always be predicted by an intimate understanding of things within those systems. How could we predict such emergences? How could we predict them, when, as was suggested by physicist Werner Heisenberg's Uncertainty Principle, even at the scale of individual atoms, the building blocks of matter, there are no hard truths, only realms of probability?

How, for example, could you predict that the chaos of the Big Bang would have led to the spectacular beauty and order of spiral galaxies? How could you predict that the violent deaths of stars long gone would have seeded our own solar system, a solar system with a single, incredibly diverse planet, a planet that was neither boiling hot, nor frozen solid, a planet with a moon orbiting about it like a tetherball driving the oceanic tides, a planet with just the right mix of stability and upheaval to keep things interesting, a planet, that for some unknown reason, gave birth to life.

When I look at diagrams of the early stages of human gestation, especially during the time between weeks four and six, when the undistinguished primordial jelly bean of an embryo morphs and cleaves its way towards the most basic expression of a human form, my mind stops, unable to bridge the gap between the starting point and finish line. Life, with its steady and unyielding metamorphosis, is inconceivably outrageous!

The origin of life, indeed, is also one of those unfathomable arisings. Current estimates have the earth forming around 4.5 billion years ago, with the first billion years totally life-free. Imagine this early earth, with all its inanimate objects already in place: The Earth's surface, pummeled by asteroids and meteorites, was also driven by the heat at the core, moved about slowly, over time, building volcanoes and mountain ranges, enjoying the frequent cataclysmic events totally guilt-free. Volcanoes erupted, earthquakes rumbled, landslides ran down the mountains, tsunamis inundated the land, all with no one there to complain, or file an insurance claim, or mourn the loss of their loved ones. The oceans were filled with water, waves crashed on the shores of deserted beaches, rain fell from the sky and rivers ran in the valleys. There was change, and exchange, and interdependence.

But there was no life, at least not as biologists attempt to define it today.

Then, for some unknown reason, single-celled organisms with the capacity to convert the energy around them—perhaps the heat from thermal vents, perhaps the energy from the early sun—into food energy appeared in the early oceans. They began to multiply and thrive in an atmosphere so toxic by our standards that we would die within minutes if placed there. These organisms were super simple compared to what we have today. But like the atom was to the sub-atomic particles that precede it, based on what there was before—earth, water, fire, and air—they were *inconceivably* complex.

Even the simplest of living organisms must contain things such as proteins and enzymes which facilitate chemical reactions; it must be able to feed itself, gathering energy in some way or another to allow it to survive and to grow. And it must be able to reproduce itself, or some version of itself, which requires a very specific coding mechanism shared by all life forms, known as DNA.

DNA not only stores the genetic code responsible for the characteristics of an organism, it also has the ability to manifest, to give form to the codes stored within. An incredibly complex structure consisting of two interwoven spirals connected by molecular rungs, so vastly complex compared to anything found outside the living world that the likelihood of the disorganized molecules of some lifeless primordial soup combining in such a way is next to none, an observation that prompted DNA co-discoverer, Nobel Prize winner Francis Crick, to speculate about its origin as possibly extraterrestrial.

But it happened. And no one can say for sure why. For the sake of our own explorations on the Ground of Creativity, it is not important that we solve such a mystery, only that we acknowledge it and feel the weight of the mystery itself. As far we know, the planet on which we live was once devoid of life. And now, for some unknown reason, it teems with it.

Finally, following the wild and crazy ride of the evolution of life on our planet up to the relatively recent past, we have the emergence of consciousness, specifically conscious self-awareness, our single most defining characteristic as human beings. Whereas the planet has been around for some four billion years, and life has been around for three billion years, scientists speculate that it has only been in the last several hundred thousand years that conscious self-awareness has emerged.

Before we go on, it is important to note that almost all of the world's religious and spiritual traditions have different views of the origins of consciousness. Whereas the scientific view is a bottom up approach, speculating that consciousness emerged from more and more complex organizations of inanimate matter, the traditions overwhelmingly favor a top down approach, seeing that the most pervasive primordial substance of the universe was not inanimate matter, but an animated awareness. Taoists, for example, posit that the unknowable *Tao* which permeates everything led to the expression of *yin* and *yang*, the feminine and masculine energies, respectively, which, in turn, led to the manifest world as we know it with all its brilliance and variety, including humans. In the Abrahamic traditions— Judaism, Christianity, and Islam—the universe was created by the Creator, and that Creator's awareness was absolute.

Even Buddhists, who hold a non-theistic, cyclical view of the universe, a universe that is constantly arising, abiding, and ceasing, have similar ideas about the role of awareness in forming the universe as we know it. Buddhists speculate that it is the karma of the previous manifestation of the universe—that is the conscious imprint of the beings that inhabited it—that set the current universe in motion. It is karma, all the unresolved narratives of those previous beings, that causes the cosmic winds to blow and, in time, bring the new universe into being.

In other words, according to the spiritual traditions, consciousness doesn't arise from matter; matter precipitates out of consciousness. And in an instant, or over billions of years, once awareness took its form as conscious self-awareness, instincts, mutations, and the survival of the physically fittest were no longer the only game in town. Creativity as a path walked by an individual became a reality.

Allowing all the cards to be on the table, allowing the best of what we know from the objective observations of science and the best of what we know from subjective experiences of sages and seekers since time immemorial, let's take a moment to imagine conscious self-awareness awakening in that first unknown individual. Whether the fruition of conscious self-awareness began at the bottom of the ocean or was precipitated from the vastness of space, what would it have been like for somebody in our universe, or at least in our tiny neck of the woods for the very first time, to be suddenly endowed with the capacity to make real choices, to remember the past and imagine the future, and to see itself in the mirror?

Imagine: It's early morning in a wide, stepped river valley. Before nightfall, someone or something wedged its way into a crevasse in a rock outcropping near the summit, instinctively settling there for a bit of warmth and protection, sleeping fitfully during the long, cold night.

It's unclear whether this creature is male or female, or perhaps a newborn birthed during the night. It's unclear whether or not the creature ate something unusual before going to bed or was injured by one of the many predators that roam these lands. It's unclear if the creature dreamt of something significant during the night, or if the creature even possessed the capacity to dream in the first place. It's also unclear whether the creature is of sound health—a model example of their own species—or some sort of strange mutation, a mutation rejected by their own brethren but destined to change the world.

What is certain is that the outlook of the one who bears witness to the dawn on this particular morning is remarkably different from the outlook of the one who went to sleep in the evening. Not only is the creature aware of its surroundings and of itself, but it is also *aware of being aware* of its surroundings. This creature is also *aware of being aware* of their own internal experience, including the miraculous complexity of thoughts and feelings. This creature awakes not only to the feel of the cold morning air and the visual contrasts of light and darkness, but to a new umbrella awareness that includes an abstract sense of time, the desire to be warmer and the capacity to do something about it, and a new and profound recognition of the staggering beauty of the coming of day.

For the first time on the history of the planet, not only is it the dawn of the day, it is the dawn of conscious self-awareness itself in a particular species, a newly emergent awareness with incredible capacities and awesome potentials, an awareness that you and I have inherited from our ancestors, an awareness we continue to utilize and wrestle with today.

In actuality, we have no way of knowing the details of how conscious self-awareness came about. It is another critical component of our capacity to create, which is deeply shrouded in mystery. Perhaps it came about like the ever-changing surface of the earth; each tiny raindrop moving a grain of sand downslope, each massive asteroid closing the curtain on one act of the play and resetting the stage for another. Perhaps it came about like a bolt of lightning, charges building up on both the land and sky until they reach a critical point, and united. In the way many of us enjoy music without any musical training, the exact details of the story aren't as important as the felt sense of the significance of the story itself.

It is important to note that aspects of consciousness were already in place. Plants, insects, and animals had all developed sophisticated ways of communicating with one another long before we came on the scene. Plants communicate through the release of invisible chemicals that act as love letters, cease and desist letters, boundary setting letters, and messages of simply being. Bees had long been dancing about, their movements communicating the location of pollen sources to their bee brethren. Jay birds squawk to claim territory, coyotes whoop to confirm a fresh kill.

Even so-called inanimate objects have aspects of consciousness. All material objects, for example, feel the pull of gravity acting on them. Charged particles have a certain consciousness that determines how they behave in a magnetic field. In its liquid state, the iron in molten lava, for example, orients itself to the Earth's magnetic field before it cools and turns into rock. An atom has prescribed preferences known as "quantum" that determine where an electron can and cannot orbit. The molecules in quartz crystals have a consciousness of the underlying molecular structure, a structure that through growth and repetition, repeats itself at a scale visible to the naked eye. A rubber band has a memory of sorts that allows it to return to its original shape.

But nothing in the natural world comes close to the plasticity and adaptability of the human mind. The brain, the principle organ responsible for conscious self-awareness, is itself an accretion of the adaptations and advancements of earlier life forms. In sharing the dynamic, interdependent aspects of our universe, it's not a single thing, but many brains really. Like layers of an onion, each human brain contains a reptilian brainstem, surround by a paleo (old) mammalian cortex, surrounded by a neo-mammalian cortex, each one marking a different period of planetary evolution, from dinosaurs to mammals to early primates such as chimpanzees. And the two outermost layers are further divided into two hemispheres, each with remarkably distinct qualities, connected by a bridge, the corpus callosum, which allows for communication between the two halves.

More than any other species, the agility of our minds is dependent upon a long period of protection and nurturing during our early years of infancy and early childhood. We aren't born into the world fully formed. We aren't able to hit the ground running. We are intensely dependent upon others from the beginning of our lives to the end. This period of helplessness is essential for our creativity, for without it, we would simply respond instinctively to different situations as they presented themselves. Our post-utero, extended gestation allows our brain to wire itself not just once but many times over throughout our lifetime. Though each and every one us have our habits, preferences, and idiosyncrasies, we are not robots playing out pre-programmed scripts. We are constantly changing and evolving, allowing outdated ideas, unhealthy situations, and self-defeating habits to die out and new, healthier, more expansive ones to emerge, all the while having the unique capacity to connect deeply with the world on a variety of very different levels, the level of the senses, of emotion, of thoughts, and at levels that seem to defy any satisfactory description.

Though our initial helplessness as infants and toddlers may go away, at least during the middle portion of our lives, we are and remain intensely dependent on others and the world around us to fulfill both our most basic needs on up to our most profound desires and wishes. This sense of connection is not only essential to our physical and emotional well-being, it is crucial for us to be able to create anything at all. Through both our passive sense of connection to the world around us—opening up and allowing the world to enter our mind stream—and our active sense of connection—our willingness to go out into the world with intentions and goals and to test our capabilities—our vibrant, living relationship to the defining aspects of the Ground of Creativity, luminous dynamism, miraculous interdependence, and mysterious complexity—gives us the barometers by which we feel into our own creative capacities. The natural cycles of our own creative efforts—expansion and contraction, awaiting, becoming, abiding, and ceasing; birth and death, stabilization and falling apart—all become portals for connecting with the creative universe ever more deeply.

All of which debunks the third myth of creativity, that it is inherent to some activities, such as art and music, but not to others, such as science and engineering. Since mysterious complexity is a defining characteristic of the creative universe and has given rise to confounding impossibilities such as life and conscious self-awareness, and since all of our uniquely human activities are based on these impossibilities, every act and every undertaking can be experienced as a manifestation of unceasing creativity. Since every moment of our lives is the result of luminous dynamism, miraculous interplay, and mysterious complexity, every moment of our lives is an opportunity to create, to connect with the world around us, to be filled with wonder, and, in turn, to affect it in a meaningful way.

You Are the Creative Universe

It's all in you, packed, simply packed, more atoms than all the stars in the heavens, a trillion cells that divided from just two, the story of the universe pervading every one of those cells, the solidity of earth in your bones, the fluidity of water in your veins, the fire of the sun in your heart, the movement of air in your lungs, the infinity of space in your imagination, all working together, blood and bile, muscles and ligaments, enzymes and bacteria, synapse and grey matter, all working together to support your wide range of sensations and emotions, thoughts and feelings, allowing you that rare and powerful sense of who you are, that capacity to ponder your place in the world and to unveil your unique and timely gifts, waiting, just waiting, for your hands upon the clay, your feet upon the dance floor, the song within your throat, the equation in your mind, your fingers on the keyboard, the vision channeled, the message delivered, and *voila!*

The story of the universe continues.

The Ground of Creativity is none other than the universe itself, experienced for what it is. This universe is a creative universe, a dynamic, interdependent, astonishing universe. It is not just something we inhabit. It is not like a new home that we move to from some other place. The whole of the universe has given birth to each and every one of us. From the calcium atoms that make up our bones, to the emotions that reconfigure our faces, from the blood that runs in our veins, to the thoughts that dance in our heads, to the dreams that confound us at night, all are end products of an epic journey that began with beginningless time and continues into this very moment.

We are both inhabitants and products of the universe, and as products *we reflect the universe in everything we do*. From the cataclysmic beginning, through the formation of the first atoms, and the gathering of those first atoms into stars, through the forging of the original atoms into new ones at the nuclear foundries at the centers of stars, through the behemoth explosions of the stars and the seeding of the universe with a richer, more colorful palette, all this has miraculously, over billions of years, given rise to life, then to conscious self-awareness, and, most recently, to you and me. In this very moment, we sit at the farthest outreaches of the story of the universe (at least in our localized sphere) with the long drama of the human influence—prehistoric, ancient civilization, Middle Ages, modern and post modern—being like a single sheet of rice paper atop a mighty mountain.

Since the universe is inherently creative, constantly reinventing itself moment after moment, and since we have arisen as a part of this universe, we too are naturally creative. Simply put, creativity is our birthright.

For now let's deepen our relationship to the Ground of Creativity by welcoming the luminous dynamism as it expresses itself in all our life's changes, both those we desire and those we do not. Let's deepen our relationship by experiencing the miraculous interdependence that has given rise to each and every one of us as well as the richness and brilliance of the world we inhabit. Finally, and perhaps most importantly, let's deepen our relationship to the Ground of Creativity by diving headlong into the mysterious complexity of it all, the unknowable mysteries of the world which have given birth to matter, to life, and to conscious self-awareness, feeling the weight and levity of the questions themselves, learning to abide in those pregnant, unanswerable spaces and feel the awesome creative potential they hold.

By doing this, we draw on an inexhaustible wellspring of creativity, and we also appreciate the necessary cycles and challenges of an ongoing creative life.

PART TWO

THE PATH OF CREATIVITY

CULTIVATING INSIGHT: ISAAC NEWTON AND THE LAW OF UNIVERSAL GRAVITATION

...see the rose through world-colored glasses.
—*Lawrence Ferlinghetti*

In the spring of 1665, with an outbreak of the bubonic plague beginning to sweep over London, Cambridge University elected to close its doors, sending thousands of students home to their families, among them a recent graduate of the prestigious Trinity College named Isaac Newton.

It must have been hugely disappointing for the 22-year-old to return to the family farm in Lincolnshire County. While Newton had excelled as an undergraduate and was anxious to continue his studies, his family life left a lot to be desired. His father died before Newton was born. His mother married a minister and abandoned Newton at the age of three, only to return eight years later with three step-siblings in tow. By then Newton had been attending school since the age of five, and demonstrated remarkable aptitudes for drawing and assembling mechanical devices. But his mother removed him from his inventive tinkering, forcing the budding 11-year-old scholar to work the land, which he deeply resented.

Far from the university and back with his unsupportive family, Newton continued to explore. In his 18 months on the farm, he came up with the seeds of four groundbreaking discoveries that would forever change our understanding of the natural world, discoveries that were crucial to physics, mathematics, astronomy, and optics, discoveries which helped usher in the age of modern science, discoveries so significant that many still to this day consider Newton to be the greatest scientist who ever lived.

What was it about this particular person, at that particular place, in that particular time that led to such seminal discoveries? More importantly, what can we learn from the situation in order to cultivate our own creative insights?

The quintessence of creativity is the *experience* of insight. Insight is a distinct and coveted type of knowing, a knowing marked by a seeming departure from our conventional experience of the world, a knowing that leaps into new realms of liveliness and possibility, a knowing that seems to rise above the limitations of a perspective we held just moments before. It is the ability to apprehend in a way that words cannot adequately describe. It is a type of understanding that transcends reason, an immediate and intuitive knowing that is irrefutable to the person having the experience and difficult if not impossible to convey to others.

In modern science, the experience of insight falls under the category of "divergent thinking," meaning that the inner mental experience seems to diverge from our normal ways of thinking. In my experience, this is an understatement. As an airplane is to a track-bound train, the experience of insight doesn't just jump the tracks of thought, it seems to rise above thinking all together, allowing us to see the world in a whole new way.

Insight describes our initial inspiration to take on a project, as well as those moments of clarity that allow us to move forward with a sense of courage, connection, expansion, and growth. Beyond what we circumscribe as our "creative pursuits," insight describes those powerful and unmistakable moments of clarity that open us up and allow us to "see" beyond both our prevailing beliefs and the throng of endless details that sometimes cloud our natural awareness and receptivity. Insight illuminates our purpose in life and provides nourishment along our journey to carry it out.

Insightful experiences come in many forms. Like a basketball player adjusting his course to the movement of the defender in front of him, insights can describe subtle, instinctive shifts in our awareness which tweak our course of action toward a more favorable direction, shifts which fly just at the border of conscious awareness. Insights can be brief moments of clarity that stop our unexamined momentum and cause us to look at other options that in hindsight seem to have made all the difference in the success of our project. Insights can take the form of sudden breakthroughs after weeks or months of dead end struggles and mental constipation when suddenly a clear path is laid out before us. And, most profoundly, insights can include life-changing events, ones that engulf us completely, ones that merge all aspects of our being with the world around us, ones that change us forever, and ones we never forget. In any case, be it a barely audible whisper or an emphatic roar, the *Ah-ha!* of insight is both the felt sense of the creative life force welling up inside us and our desire to share it with others.

Insightful experiences arise from a wide variety of situations, both pleasurable and painful. The precursors and catalysts of insights, however, are often hard to identify and can seem random and unpredictable. Like a crystal suddenly precipitating out of a solution or a cloud emerging from a clear blue sky, insights seem to appear out of nowhere, adding to their mysterious intrigue.

But arise they do, cutting through darkness, shedding welcomed light on our situation, and illuminating both the present moment as well as the road ahead of us. Insightful experiences can arise out of grand perspectives, like the view afforded an astronaut looking down at the world from space. They can result from penetrating experiences in nature, like a surfer running his fingers along a wall of water deep inside a barreling wave. They can be sparked by the flippant remarks of total strangers or the revelatory confessions of lifelong friends. They can come about during sensual experiences, like taking our first bite of a reverently prepared saffron rice dish with pistachio sauce. They can also involve changes in our emotions, arising from both nuanced shifts in our sense of well-being and cataclysmic ruptures accompanying life-changing events, both of which create gaps in our assumptions, creating space for fresh perspective. Insights can arise out of the experience of hitting "rock bottom," when you find yourself finally breaking down out after a long decline of mishaps, failure, and fiascos. And, perhaps most curiously, they can spring forth in the most ordinary of moments when, for example, we are taking out the garbage and are suddenly overcome with an unexplainable feeling of peace.

But none of these situations—neither grand perspectives, nor time spent in nature, nor penetrating sensorial experiences, nor humiliating fiascos—*guarantees* the experience of insight, which returns us to our original question: What are the underlying qualities of creative insight and how can we cultivate them?

Experiencing Insight

Of the four discoveries Newton made while working the family farm, the most legendary was the one leading to the Law of Universal Gravitation. As the story goes, Newton sat in his family's apple orchard, his back to the trunk of a tree, a canopy of apples above him, looking at the distant moon.

Years later, in recalling the events of that day, Newton would describe his mood as "contemplative," a mood that was "occasioned by the fall of an apple." At that moment, Newton intuited that the force drawing the apple towards the earth and the force keeping the moon in orbit were the same.

Newton's intuition ran contrary to the prevailing view. In those days it was presumed that the laws governing earth and the laws governing the heavens had to be fundamentally different. After all, the Earth was the realm of humankind, whereas the heavens were the Kingdom of God. Why would anyone work to secure their place in Heaven if it were governed by the same laws creating the toil and strife on Earth? Why would anyone work to secure their place if it were subject to the same gruesome tragedies as the Black Death sweeping over London?

In that moment, however, while sitting in his family orchard, contemplating the moon hanging in the sky, then witnessing a single apple falling to the ground, Newton *experienced* the force acting upon them as one and the same.

The most important thing to know about insights is that *we all experience them*. It doesn't matter where you grew up, or how old you are, or what your level of education might be. It doesn't matter if you spend your time installing air-conditioning units, or writing legal letters, or handing out parking tickets, insights are an integral part of your experience as a human being. It doesn't even matter if you see yourself as particularly creative or not. Insights come with your innate and intrinsic awareness.

I should clarify the difference between 1) insightful ideas 2) the experience of insight. Insightful ideas, such as Einstein's *Theory of Relativity*, or artist Jeff Koon's decision to make metal sculptures simulating balloon animals, even the religious ideas such as "love thy neighbor" are all *results*, end products of something much more basic and profound. All these insightful ideas were preceded by an *experience*, an experience beyond what words can adequately describe, a moment of profound connection, or alignment, or awe, an indescribable feeling of irrefutable truth. The experience may endure for only a split second, but it is essential because it creates an opening in our stream of consciousness for something entirely fresh. If you take just one thing from this section, let it be this: Insightful *ideas* come from insightful *experiences*, not the other way around.

In this context, "try to think creatively" is the worst advice we could give someone, as it will have them barking up the wrong tree. Why? Because thinking tends to recycle the material that is already present in a person's mind, creating a wall of white noise, a buzz of discursive information, a static that inhibits our ability to relate to the world in a way that is fresh. As our reasoning mind cinches down around a problem, scrutinizing it from every angle, determined to know the answer, we are actually lessening the possibility of a fortuitous opening; we're actually inhibiting the experience of insight.

Along these lines, South African artist and animated film maker William Kentridge has this to say about his process, "All the interesting ideas I've ever had, all the interesting work I've done, has always been against ideas I've had. It's always happening in between the things I thought I was doing that the real work has happened."

The process of cultivating insights involves 1) creating certain conditions that 2) lead to insightful experiences that 3) have the *possibility* of being developed into insightful ideas. Cultivating insight, then, should not be viewed as an exercise in cultivating fully formed ideas. Think of it instead as an exercise in cultivating gaps and openings, an exercise in tilling last winter's hardpan so that new seeds can take hold, an exercise in setting up the situations that lead to those types of experience that either fly below the radar of fully formed ideas or transcend them all together. Insights, true insights, are *experiences*, full-body, full-being experiences that seem, if only for a split second, to merge your awareness with the entire world around you. And in this merging—where you the perceiver and the world you perceive become one—insights describe a direct and immediate way of knowing, a knowing that is different than your ability to reason. In the words of painter Ran Ortner, whose dynamic paintings capture the timeless becoming of the sea, "Humans are deeply emotional beings. We don't rationalize our way into love; we fall. We don't rationalize our way into the richest experiences; we get swept away."

Compare the experience of insight to the more conventional way of being in the world. Those of us who have been educated in the modern West tend to view ourselves as discrete individuals that are separate from the world around us, including other people. The experience of insight, however, junks that whole perspective, dissolving any perceived sense of separation, rooting us firmly in the present, fully immersing us in a creative conundrum. Then, from the inside, and with all sense of separation dissolved, an experience of unity reveals exactly what we need to know with striking clarity.

Like a raindrop falling into the ocean, the experience of insight gives us access to a type of awareness that is both vast and curiously familiar, a homecoming of sorts, and one that reveals an irrefutable, felt sense of truth. Like the actor channeling the spirit of his character or a skilled copywriter who intuits the unique desires of one person in her target audience, or even a subatomic physicist dropping into the experience of being a tiny lepton, the experience of insight dissolves the barriers between ourselves and the world around us.

Insights can lead to ideas, concepts, images, and new and fruitful directions in all aspects of our lives, but as *experiences*—as nonconceptual experiences which are sometimes sensorial, sometimes transcendent, sometimes a combination of both—insights themselves remain *unrepeatable* and largely *indescribable* to others. As experiences happening within the individual, they can't be copied down on paper, stuck in an envelope, or mailed to a person in the next county. They can't be captured on film nor recorded with a microphone. They can't be explained by the greatest of orators, nor acted out by the most skilled of thespians, nor quantified by the savviest of mathematicians. No sculptor can give them form; no engineer can replicate their function. They cannot be commoditized, nor traded, nor guarded in a vault. Like the *experience* of eating chocolate ice cream or the *experience* of watching the moon rise, or the experience of watching that same moon hanging in the sky and suddenly having an apple fall beside you, the experience of insight can be held by no one. Like a gust of wind coming down from the mountaintop, insightful experiences ruffle the leaves of our awareness and pry at our foundations for a moment, and then are gone, leaving us with the challenge of *interpreting* them in a way that we can begin to share with others.

Furthermore, insightful experiences do not occur in isolation. They are the essence of interdependence, involving the union of an individual's awareness with a particular place, within a particular context, at a particular time. Like a lock whose tumblers are loosened by the unrepeatable qualities of one particular key, the experience of insight is like opening a cosmic doorway, the opening itself inviting something completely nourishing and inarguably true for the person who opens that door. Insightful experiences seem to hold universal truths, yet are deeply personal, landing in a very particular way for the person who experiences them.

To recap, insights are 1) *experiences* that 2) *all of us have* that 3) involve a *sense of interdependence*. They are not ideas or concepts, they aren't something foreign to our experience, and they don't occur in isolation.

FIVE QUALITIES OF INSIGHTFUL EXPERIENCES

As experiences occurring within one person, within one particular context, insights share five defining qualities: **ineffability, certainty, brevity, receptivity, and individuality.**

Ineffability points to the heart of the experience of insight. We *feel* how profound insights can be, we *intuit* how they stand out from our ordinary experience, we are *moved* by the felt sense of unity, but we have no way of sharing that experience *directly* with others. Since the experience of insight transcends reason, our language always comes up short, making the experience itself *indescribable*.

The quality of ineffability is accompanied by an unexplainable **certainty,** a sense of truth that accompanies the experience, a truth that satisfies our desire for understanding while defying immediate

63

intellectual comprehension. Furthermore, our certainty may feel so profound and so personal that we may even be hesitant to share it, fearing others might misinterpret or misconstrue it in some way, or flatly reject it.

The experience of insight is usually **brief**, though it may strongly influence our way of approaching our lives for days, weeks, or years afterward. It may be an experience so penetrating and profound that it guides us for the rest of our lives. But the experience itself, like a flash of lightning, usually lasts only a short while—a few moments to several hours and in rare instances, several consecutive days.

The experience of insight is also a passive experience, one of **receptivity.** Though we may have some sense of preparing ourselves or making an effort before the experience, insight, ultimately, is something we *receive*. As is commonly expressed in statements such as "Suddenly it dawned on me," or "I was struck by...," insights feel as though they are coming to us or through us. Receptivity within our reigning cultural context—one that stresses productivity and taking action—presents one of the biggest conundrums to the cultivation of insight: How does one become open to passively receive?

Finally, the experience of insight is deeply personal, giving it the quality of **individuality.** Although insights appear with the perception of universal truths, they are preciously intimate—they are experienced by you, the individual, and only you. Two people could be in the exact same situation at the exact same time, and one might experience a life-changing insight whereas the other might experience "business as usual," just another ordinary moment no different most others. Some people, for example, step to the edge of the Grand Canyon and are moved to tears by its expansiveness. Others step to the edge and feel boredom and disappointment. Some have insightful experiences prompted by symbols on a blackboard, where others see only gibberish. The insight itself, then, reflects a coming together of some unique and timely aspect within us that is ready to connect with a person, place, or situation that is ripe to affect us in some unforeseen way.

Furthermore, the interpretation of the insightful experience within ourselves, as well as our attempts to explain it to others (which now involves memory rooted in language), will be filtered through our unique history as an individual and the influences of our upbringing, the prevalent culture, and a whole host of other factors. Depending on who we are and where we are in our lives, we might interpret a similar insightful experience as either a sign to change course or as a reassurance to continue full steam ahead. The truths we perceive and the consequences of bringing them into the world (or guarding them if we so choose) are fully our own.

Newton's legendary experience in the apple orchard demonstrates all the qualities of insight. First , he was away from his beloved learning environment and seeking, perhaps, a bit of respite from the difficulties of his family relationships. There, in the orchard, the ineffability was evident in his contemplative mood, a mood suggesting a departure from the use of his keen intellect, a mood suggesting a meditative, even mystical quality to his mindset. Next, the experience established an intriguing link between two very different objects, one celestial, the other terrestrial, the link itself describing an unforeseen truth (certainty), a truth running counter to the widely held beliefs of the day.

More popular accounts of that fortuitous day have the apple actually landing on Newton's head. This appears to be more lore than fact. In all likelihood, the apple didn't fall on Newton, but its *significance* most certainly did. In that brief moment (brevity), the seed insight that would become the Law of Universal Gravitation wasn't something Newton sought out; it came to him, metaphorically striking him on the head (passivity).

Finally, the significance of the apple falling didn't strike just anyone. Had the mother or one of the half-siblings seen that same apple fall while Newton was behind the barn splitting wood, the world today might look a whole lot different. The significance was personal: It struck one young man named Isaac Newton (individuality), a person, like each and every one of us, with his own unique history and particular set of aptitudes, interests, and outlooks.

INSIGHTS ALONG THE PATH

The experience of insight, albeit strange and wonderful, is a natural part of being human. Like throwing back the curtains to experience the morning sunshine, the experience of insight merges our finite sense of who we are with something much, much larger.

The frequency and profundity of insightful experiences, however, vary greatly among individuals. Some of us may feel overwhelmed by an abundance of insightful experiences, and find ourselves chasing one creative hunch after the next like leaves in a wind storm. For others of us, insights seem to happen but once in a great while. Still others of us have plenty of insightful experiences but don't value them, believing that they are outlandish, stupid, or that they don't seem to measure up to others we deem "more creative" than ourselves. And for many of us, insightful experiences seem completely elusive, a deadbeat muse that refuses to visit, a coveted and time-honored aptitude of people more fortunate than us.

As you are well aware at this point, your miraculous capacities to think, feel, and do are already in place. And whether or not you acknowledge it, you are a product of an amazingly dynamic, interdependent, deeply mysterious, and fabulously creative universe; whether you acknowledge it or not, you contribute to the arising of the universe moment after moment. So, the question to ask is: What prevents you from experiencing the nourishment of insight and the fulfillment of creativity as a regular part of your life?

When it comes to insights and to creativity in general, the Path of Creativity begins first and foremost by acknowledging that *creativity is a journey and not a destination*. It is dynamic, not static. Since the universe is interdependent and ever-changing, the hope of arriving at some sort of final destination, including an unending stream of insight, goes against the very nature of the creative universe we inhabit. As soon as we arrive in one seemingly fortuitous place, the world changes around us. That place may be right where we want to be for decades, or it may begin to stink like a sneaker moments after arrival. The point isn't to favor take-offs over landings, or cutting ties to growing roots, but to flow, and adapt, and to learn from all situations as they arise. We may arrive at places with wide open vistas and others that are downright claustrophobic. When we commit to living a creative life, all experiences are valued stepping stones along our lifelong creative journey; when met with wonder and the willingness to learn, all experiences become valuable teachers.

Next, we begin to *assess our present relationship to the Ground of Creativity with unabashed honesty*. How do we experience luminous dynamism, miraculous interplay, and mysterious complexity in our own lives? Do we accept them fully or do we reject them in some way, thinking we can somehow stop the cogs of the universe when we get things to line up to our liking? Are we comfortable with the idea of change but not so keen on interdependence, preferring instead to view ourselves as self-made men and women? How about all those unknowns out there? Instead of relaxing into them, are we spending energy trying to explain them away somehow? Or perhaps we numb ourselves to avoid feeling into the fear of all we don't know? Though the Ground of Creativity is always at work, it is essential that we are honest about which aspects we accept and which we reject by looking at our habits and behaviors. The more we find ourselves tuned into the workings of the Ground of Creativity, the more we will experience creativity as a natural expression of living.

Then, we begin actively deepening our relationship to the Ground of Creativity by cultivating certain practices that undermine our tendency to disconnect from our direct experience of the world around us. In an age flooded with information in the form of texts, emails, digital avatars, marketing, spam, junk mail, and other info-noise, this is essential. We can drive across a crowded city, for example, flipping through radio stations, pondering an idea for a new blog post, sipping a cup of coffee, and still, somehow, manage to arrive safely. The cultivation of insight, however, requires us to *pay attention to what we are doing while we are doing it*, taking our thinking mind's ability to wander off into virtual worlds, and refocus it on the utter miraculousness of ordinary experiences. In other words, we take off the rose-colored glasses or abandon our sob stories of unending tragedies and start to pay closer attention to this life we are living just as it is. As Julia Cameron, author of the immensely popular book *The Artist's Way*, said, "People frequently believe the creative life is grounded in fantasy. The more difficult truth is that creativity is grounded in reality..."

The Path of Creativity and the cultivation of insight unfold in different ways for different people. In general, for those who are willing to walk it, the progress is sometimes slow, sometimes rapid, but ultimately, deeply rewarding. No matter where you may sit on the spectrum of insight, by deepening your relationship to the Ground of Creativity, *by deepening your commitment to reality*, you will steadily gain confidence in your creative capacities and expand your felt sense of wholeness, significance, meaning, and purpose. The seed that would become the Universal Law of Gravitation, for example, was planted in an instant in young Isaac Newton's mind. But it took over two decades for him to develop and publish his findings.

For those of you who do not put in the effort, there may be little progress over time. Insights will still arrive at your doorstep. But once the flash is over and you return to your normal state of being, the insights may be more haunting than helpful. Instead of beacons or sign posts guiding your ongoing efforts to deepen your intimacy with the Ground of Creativity—that is, with the luminous dynamism, miraculous interdependence, and mysterious complexity that underlies our universe—the insights may feel like strange and confounding aberrations. Or you may confuse the insight as a sort of ultimate destination and not a sign post guiding you along. "At last I have arrived!" you may declare, only to realize that the oasis was but a mirage. Without committing to the Path of Creativity, without your commitment to reestablishing your connection to the Ground of Creativity again and again, once the flash is over, you may be left feeling confused and bewildered about how to fit such a vast sense of connection into your "normal," seemingly isolated life.

As for Isaac Newton, his experience in the apple orchard at his family farm in Lincolnshire County would prove to be a giant step forward in advancing our scientific understanding of the universe. In time, he left the farm and returned to Trinity College. There, over the next two decades, he would develop his insightful experience into the Law of Universal Gravitation, publishing his findings in 1687 in his now famous book, *Principia Mathematic*. Not insignificantly, that book also contained the three universal laws of motion and advanced every branch of known mathematics, instantly becoming the standard for scientific writing and, some years later, the guidebook driving the mechanics of the Industrial Revolution. To this day, his work is still the foundation of classical physics.

The impact of *Principia Mathematic* propelled Isaac Newton into the international spotlight. He earned privileged government positions, was knighted by Queen Anne in 1705, and, upon his death, was buried in Westminster Abbey. His epitaph, penned by the British poet Alexander Pope, read:

Nature and nature's laws lay hid in night; God said "Let Newton be" and all was light.

Despite his fame, Isaac Newton was modest about his own achievements. As a true creator, he was more interested in the lifelong journey of creativity. Instead of resting on his laurels, he applied his abilities wherever he could. Later on in life, even when he was given powerful yet cushy positions for his previous achievements, he continuously applied himself, drawn on by his remarkable curiosity and reverence for the world around him.

Another key in understanding the remarkable life of Isaac Newton, and something we can all adapt if we desire to live a creative life, can be discovered in how he viewed his own relationship to the world. In essence, Newton saw himself as part of something much larger than himself, and his valued discoveries and contributions just a playful part of that. He maintained an appreciation for the mystery inherent in all of creation. Late in his life he wrote:

I do not know what I may appear to the world, but to myself I seem to have been only like a boy playing on the sea-shore, and diverting myself in now and then finding a smoother pebble or a prettier shell than ordinary, whilst the great ocean of truth lay all undiscovered before me.

MANIFESTATION:
CHRISTO, JEANNE-CLAUDE, AND RUNNING FENCE

The strongest man in the world can't even lift his own leg.
—*Traditional Zen Koan*

In the early 1970s, with the Vietnam War drawing to a close and the OPEC oil crisis tanking the U.S. economy, a Manhattan-based artist couple descended upon the coastal hills north of San Francisco with a $3 million budget and an outrageously ambitious plan. Inspired by snow fences they'd seen near the Continental Divide, fences designed to prevent snow drifts from overrunning mountainous highways, they wanted to erect a temporary, 18-foot high, 24.5-mile-long fabric structure that would connect the defining aspects of the California coast, unifying it by what they described as a single "ribbon of light." They called the project "Running Fence," and, like any good fence, before a single post hole was dug, it created a clear and distinct boundary between the locals, with those in favor of the project and those against it gathering in force on either side.

Born on the same day in different parts of Europe, the couple was in their mid-thirties at the time. The husband was a brash, long-haired Bulgarian-born sculptor who went by the single name Christo. His wife, Jeanne-Claude, was a chain-smoking French native and philosophy major with a knack for public relations. The two had met in Paris nearly 15 years earlier and were as determined as they were inseparable. By the time they came to California, they'd already completed a number of large-scale, high-profile art installations, including wrapping a million square feet of the Australian coast in erosion-control fabric and stringing an enormous orange curtain between two mountains near Rifle, Colorado.

But Running Fence took things to a whole new level. As it was drawn on the map, the fence wasn't to be a straight shot from east to west, but was to meander about, connecting signature features of the California coast. For Christo and Jeanne-Claude, those signature features included rural, suburban and urban spaces, the ocean, and, perhaps the essential element of the California landscape, the freeway, specifically Highway 101. To accomplish this, the proposed project would have to cross land in both Marin and Sonoma counties, requiring separate approval from each county. Along its route, the artists envisioned the fence passing through the center of the small town of Valley Ford, crossing 14 state roads and 59 privately owned ranches, and, on its western end, diving into Bodega Bay, all of which would require the approval of the California Highway Department, the California Patrol, the California Coastal Commission, and each of the individual land owners.

There were also significant engineering challenges. Due to the nature of the topography and the force of the afternoon onshore winds whipping over the mostly treeless landscape, the project would require 2050 21-foot-long steel poles driven three feet into the earth, each pole laterally braced by guy wires and a total of 14,000 earth anchors, 90 miles of steel cable, and over two million square feet of heavy nylon fabric, enough fabric to cover over 60 football fields, secured at the top and bottom by 350,000 metal hooks.

Furthermore, the cultural landscape was a complex and some-times antagonistic mix of cattle ranchers, sheep herders, dairy farm-ers, local artists, hippies, counter-culturalists, and environmentalists. Those who settled in the area were drawn to the quiet, wide-open spaces, the broad valleys and rounded summits, but for very differ-ent reasons, reasons that caused them to keep their distance from one another in the few gathering places in the area.

Thrown into all this came the most obvious outsiders of the lot, Christo and Jeanne-Claude themselves, who, along with their for-eign accents and strange artistic desires, furthered their separateness by making their rounds with a documentary film crew in tow. As word spread about the couple's desire to erect a 24.5-mile curtain through their homelands, the locals all seemed more than a little bit confused, sometimes outright suspicious. Considering all the time and materials involved, and that the fence would be standing for only 14 days, then removed without a trace, to more than a few in those provincial, salt-of-the-earth communities the whole project seem like a colossal waste of effort.

Before the project had the possibility of being a ribbon of light, it would begin as a wall of contention, with those who were for it and those against it squaring off in the courtrooms and the local shops, indeed in people's own homes, rallying around their hopes, retract-ing into their fears and prejudices, beginning, like the fence itself, to draw their own hard-edged lines in the sand.

MANIFESTATION DEFINED

We have arrived at the active and most enduring part of the creative process, where we begin affecting the world in a meaningful way, what I call *manifestation*. To manifest means to make something clear or evident to either the senses or to the intellect. It is the act of bringing something into the world that can be readily perceived by others through its physical qualities, or, in the case of ideas, its comprehensibility.

Before we go any further, it is important to clarify what manifestation is not. In the last several years, the word manifestation has become associated with a sort of mind over matter way of willing desirable objects—a nice car, a convenient parking space for that nice car just when you need it, or a new boyfriend or girlfriend, perhaps—into being, simply by thinking about those objects over and over and drawing them toward you. This, I'm afraid, is more than a little misguided, a sort of selective memory favoring the positively "manifested" outcomes while ignoring all the times it didn't seem to work.

This is also an overly simplistic reduction of the immensity of the dynamic, interdependent, deeply mysterious nature of the universe into a form that is appealing to the finite ego. Such thinking actually squelches creativity over time because it isolates individuals, leading them to believe he or she is *controlling* the world with his or her mind. Sensing our *participation* in the reordering of wholeness moment after moment is much different than thinking we are *controlling* the outcome of the universe. Don't fool yourself: Narcissists and megalomaniacs may think they are the one in the driver's seat; true creators, however, recognize that they are always small but important collaborators in something incomprehensibly vast.

Derived from *manus*, the Latin word for hand, manifestation is the act of realizing something that others can grasp onto. Many religious traditions, for example, describe the world in which we live as *the manifest realm*. From our most basic metabolic needs for air, water, and food, to our more social needs for safety, companionship, and understanding, up to our most cherished needs for wisdom, compassion, and creativity, it is this manifest realm where we engage in an unceasing exchange with the world around us. Using the rich palette of materials the manifest realm has to offer, material such as limestone for sculptures, words for poems, and fresh greens for cooking, we deepen our connection to the world through both the process of creating as well as by presenting the fruits of our labor.

Manifestation relies primarily on convergent thinking, the active process of narrowing and refining our experience of insight, giving form to the formless. Contrary to divergent thinking, convergent thinking is very analytical, requiring us to concentrate our brain power on details, discrete objects, and deliberate conversations with other key individuals. Like the drone of a bagpipe sounding in the background of the individual notes, however, we need not abandon our openness to the Ground of Creativity entirely. Yet, differing from the qualities of insight, manifestation does require a narrowing of focus and a willingness to exert ourselves to help those insightful experiences take form in the manifest realm.

Manifestation, then, is the process of developing our insights, of taking our glimpses of the ineffable and giving them form. Should a seed idea, a feeling, or concept move through the threshold of the ungraspable and begin to germinate in the realm of the measurable, new questions arise: How much do we protect the seed and how much do we let it grown on its own? Without protection and championing, the original inspiration may be overwhelmed by the demands of value engineering, roller coaster economies, fickle clients and coworkers, or our own laziness or lack of confidence. With too much protection, we may become like tanks rolling over the landscape, ignoring others' sound advice, blinded to both opportunities and pitfalls alike, ready to unleash our wrath on anyone or anything that may wish to stand in our way. When we solidify our insights, when we lose all agility and sense of humor around what we are doing—we also lose touch with those immeasurable qualities that inspired us in the first place. Our once-intriguing insights end up becoming toxic to everyone involved.

The art of manifestation, then, is learning to develop a delicate balance between two extremes: 1) letting things go entirely and 2) forcing outcomes. This difficult balance was well apparent as Christo and Jeanne-Claude began the process of forwarding their original insights.

In 1972, the couple began pitching their idea and securing the necessary permits. Being strangers in an insular community, they were not well received. Many of the ranchers, whose work was so tied to the land, had not been much farther than San Francisco. Their approach to life was pragmatic and down to earth. The ongoing feeding and care of their animals and the constant upkeep of their properties left little time for a grandiose, seemingly useless, high-brow art project.

And ranchers and dairy farmers' daily routines couldn't have been more in opposition to the routines of the artists. The dairy farmers, for example, went to sleep at 6 p.m. to awake for the 1 a.m. milking. They were not at all pleased when the couple showed up on their doorstep at 8 p.m., waking the whole house to sell them on an art project, a project, no less, that the couple wanted to run through their grazing pastures.

The ranchers and dairy farmers weren't the only ones with grave suspicions. A small but vocal minority of local artists who'd settled in the area to work on their own projects were immediately resentful of the two, high-profile, East Coast artists impinging on their territory. Furthermore, environmentalists had real concerns about the project's impact on the land, worrying not only about the impact of construction but also the impact of the droves of spectators the project would surely draw from the Bay Area, especially during peak fire season. A single carelessly flicked cigarette in the wild hands of the bracing winds could easily overrun vast tracts of land.

The locals also worried about how Running Fence might affect their home in the long run. Would it pave the way for other public spectacles such as carnivals, motorcycle rallies, and rock concerts? It had only been three years since the infamous Altamont Free Concert, which took place at another nearby Bay Area outpost, devolved into total mayhem, resulting in considerable property damage, three deaths, and one brutal murder by a member the group hired as security for the event, The Hell's Angels.

Or would the fence usher in the beginnings of a regional real estate development snapping up the open space, overtaking the land and building tract homes for Bay Area commuters? For those who relied on their land for their livelihood and for those who loved it for its provincial, sleepy-time qualities, these were genuine concerns.

As the permitting began, the first thing to be contested by the locals was the validity of the project itself. What was so artful about erecting an oversized structure that seemed little more than a glorified laundry line?

In one instance, captured by the documentary film crew at what looks like a local fairgrounds, a virulent young man squares off against a stubborn old-timer, a crowd around them jeering the two of them on.

"It's all a bunch of garbage!" yells the young man, arms flying. "That's *ART*?! Some lousy curtain with a bunch of city slickers looking at it? To *HELL* with it! I'm against it. I think it's *STUPID*!"

The old man, held back by his years but not by his outrage, shouts back, "This guy's spending $2 million in the county of Sonoma, and he's not taking anything out. He's putting money *in* here!"

"What kind of art is that? What art is that hanging a piece of rag up for 50 miles? I can hang a rag up! I bet he can't even paint a picture. He's an *IDIOT!*"

In another instance a man at a public hearing, who, based on his derby hat, satiny tie, suspenders, and a necklace of Mardi Gras beads, appears to be an artist himself, takes the podium and says, "It isn't art. A curtain 10 feet long and 18 feet high isn't art. And it's not art if it's 24 miles long."

In another hearing, a rancher's wife compares the couple's vision, both its artistic value and its temporary nature, to her own experience preparing meals in the kitchen, "There was one thing said about art being temporal. Some of the meals I prepare aren't much... But *sometimes*, I go to a lot of work to prepare a meal that I think is art, it's a masterpiece. And what happens? It get's eaten up and disappears and everyone forgets about it."

Suddenly the locals were not only having to contend with the project's short – and long-term impacts, they were also waxing philosophical, debating, and often quite passionately, the difficult question: What is art?

For Christo and Jeanne Claude, the early permitting did not go well. Their project was shut down by the opposition. On the advice of a local sheep rancher who took a liking to the couple, Christo and Jeanne-Claude began going door to door, not just to sell their project, but to begin to establish trust. The couple began hanging out with the ranchers and dairy farmers on their land, touring their properties, listening to their concerns, hearing their stories, sharing time with them, and enjoying their home-grown vegetables and home-cooked meals.

Christo and Jeanne-Claude also made the rounds about town, what little town there is in that region, attending auctions, fairs, and other local events. Motivated by their earlier mistakes, Jeanne-Claude went so far as to learn everything she could about dairy farming and sheep ranching, deepening her appreciation and understanding of the landowners' daily lives.

Without a doubt, Christo and Jeanne-Claude had a vested interest in seeing their project to completion. They made their living as artists, and the coastal hills stretching from Bodega Bay to Mitchem Hill were their current canvas. In time, however, they were no longer seen as strangers by the land owners, but as real people with an odd but compelling vision, including the financial resources to carry it out and the jobs that would go with it. More deeply, the land owners were beginning to sense Christo and Jeanne-Claude's real appreciation of *their* lives, not exclusively because their art project passed through their property. Whether or not the permits were approved, there was an opportunity for people from very different backgrounds and lifestyles to share time with another, to learn and to grow.

As time wore on, those who were for Running Fence and those who were against it became more and more entrenched in their views. The main supporters were the land owners, the ranchers and dairy farmers, who, despite the risks, also had a lot to gain. Three million dollars in the 1970s equates to over $15 dollars today. Not only would the land owners be compensated financially for their work, as Christo and Jeanne Claude always did with their projects, they'd be able to keep all the valuable fencing materials that passed through their property.

On the other side was the "Committee to Stop the Running Fence," which, ironically, was started and backed primarily by the disgruntled local artists, with further backing from environmentalists. Each time Running Fence moved a step closer to its goal, the Committee to Stop the Running Fence appealed the decision.

But in the true spirit of manifestation, Christo and Jeanne-Claude accepted the process as part of their work. All the red tape, paperwork, and legalities, all the wide-ranging displays of emotion and high-spirited debates, including their own frustrations and resulting marital squabbles, were not viewed as hurdles in the way of their ultimate goal, but part and parcel of their creative process. Taking the stand at one of the packed planning meetings in Marin County, Christo explained, "The work is not only the fabric, the steel poles, and the fence. The art project is right now here. Everybody here is part of my work. If they want it or they don't want it, anyway, they are part of my work... they are an integral part of making that project."

Christo went on to say, "I feel very strongly that 20th Century art is not a single individualistic experience. It is the very deep, political, social, economic experience I live right now with everybody here. And it is nothing involved with the make-believe. That appeal [from the opposition] was not staged by me [nor] that we have emotion and fear. But, of course, that is part of my project. I very much like to live the real life."

QUALITIES OF MANIFESTATION

The manifestation phase of the creative process describes both the process of bringing insights into fruition as well as the impact the project has after the work is completed. For now, I am focusing on bringing one's insightful experiences to some sort of fruition. In this, the process of manifestation has five qualities, qualities that mirror the qualities of insight. They are **definability, flexibility, longevity, activeness,** and **communality.**

Manifestations are **definable**. Objects such as paintings, and ideas such as physics equations, even feelings that can be expressed, are all aspects of definability. In being definable they can be shared with others. Manifestations utilize languages of various sorts—oral languages, written languages, and other symbolic languages such as diagrams, mathematics, music, or computer programming languages, even gestures and body language—any way that one can actively share an idea or an experience with others.

When manifestation involves a physical object, the qualities can be listed. An architect, for example, may specify rounded black river stones to add patterns and texture to a red concrete floor. A scientist might decide to use copper instead of silver to test a new metal alloy.

When manifestation comes in the form of an idea, it can be described in a way that can be understood by at least one other person. A philosopher, for example, may refer to a well-known treatise that creates a common ground with her reader, then present a contrasting argument. A poet may invent a new word that is framed in a way that a reader can grasp both its meaning and/or feeling. But if something remains too vague, however, or cannot be understood or experienced by others, it is not in the realm of manifestation.

My own definition of definability in regards to manifestation has its limitations. I do believe that there are cases where certain extraordinary individuals, individuals who for whatever reason seem ahead of their time, present ideas that are so beyond what the general population knows as familiar that few if any are able to fully appreciate what they have to offer. In art, what comes to mind are the paintings of Van Gogh, who only sold one of his paintings during his lifetime but is now revered as the father of Expressionism. Or the little known Greek astronomer, Aristarchus of Samos, who in the 3rd Century BC posited that it was the sun and not the Earth that is the center of the known universe, a view that was rejected by more well-known thinkers of his time such as Aristotle and Ptolemy, a view that would not be verified until 18 centuries after his death. Or what about all the saints and sages throughout history who ended up crucified, poisoned, stoned to death, or burned at the stake for shining too brightly, the cultural norms or the powers that be finding their messages too threatening or disruptive to their established way of life.

Tibetan Buddhists use the word *terma* to describe treasures of knowledge hidden by realized beings in anticipation of as yet unforeseen challenges faced by future populations. In any case, it is important to realize that sometimes conditions aren't favorable for certain insights, no matter how profound or useful, to be manifested. It is simply another aspect of the strange and wondrous ways of the world in which we live.

In the case of Running Fence, the artists had a clearly defined budget, a clearly defined list of materials, and some sense of a plan to carry it all out. Even the idea of a "ribbon of light" was a conceptual manifestation of the original insight, a concept that served the artists in developing their idea as well as selling the project along the way.

While a project may be clearly defined at the outset, manifesting it also requires a sense of **flexibility**, flexibility endowed with a healthy dose of doubt. As psychologist Rollo May wrote in his book *The Courage to Create*, "We must be fully committed, but we must also be aware at the same time that we might be wrong." Because our projects, especially large ones, unfold over time and because we are not omniscient, new opportunities and new challenges will most certainly arise. If we're too rigid with our initial ideas, we will end up forcing outcomes when a situation is screaming for a different solution altogether. At the same time, if we are undisciplined and follow every new idea that comes our way, we will have real difficulty bringing our projects to a timely conclusion with any real continuity. Flexibility, then, is itself an art and requires trial, error, and humility.

Manifestation is typically the more enduring part of the creative process, giving it the quality of **longevity.** Longevity describes the difficult and sometimes laborious process of taking our insights and making them into concrete realties. Manifestations are also enduring in that they are the objects and ideas—the new plastic of the materials engineer, the songs of blues guitarists, the fragrant rose bushes planted in a specific place by the gardener—that get launched into the world, becoming a part of it, a new, shared reality for all of us to experience. In a flash, for example, you may have decided that your photographs of storm clouds will look best and best serve your theme if they are hung from the ceiling of gallery and not on the walls. Doing it, however, figuring out ways to secure them at the top and getting them all level, takes an enormous amount of time by comparison. Longevity may require more patience and perseverance than we are comfortable with. But if something, however laborious and edgy, is calling us along, in my experience it is worth it and hugely rewarding to set out in that direction, even if we fail.

The seed insight for Running Fence, for example, was born in an instant, when Christo and Jeanne-Claude were moved by the odd and compelling snow fences near the Continental Divide in the Rocky Mountains. But the transition from a snow fence in the interior of the continent to the planning and permitting of a 24.5-mile fabric curtain running across the hills and plunging into the ocean, as well as the countless hours spent in the local communities and fundraising abroad, took more than four years in all.

Although the fence was only standing for 14 days, it had lasting and far reaching effects, including its effects on me 21 years later, a first-year architecture student who first heard of Running Fence from Professor Keith Loftin in a lecture hall on the Denver campus of the University of Colorado, not too far from those original snow fences.

Manifestation is also the more **active** part of the creative process. Instead of waiting for insights to come to us, we take action, turning those insights into concrete realities. This is the time when we roll up our sleeves, don our lab coats, open our notebooks, get out our phone lists, assess our bank accounts, and get to work. We begin by taking those ineffable insights and visualizing a home for them, contemplating their gestation within time frames and budgets, sharing our insights with others with know-how pertinent to our vision.

The naming of their project "Running Fence," the scouting for a suitable location, the outlining of the fence on a map, the thousands of phone calls, the numerous trips between Manhattan and Sonoma and Marin County, all the visits in people's homes and all the meetings in the court houses, and the erection and dismantling of the fence itself were all aspects of the active nature of manifestation, all of which required considerable will and effort from Christo, Jeanne-Claude, and innumerable others, especially the ranchers and dairy farmers, who consistently attended the public hearings despite their arduous schedules.

Finally, manifestation moves a creative undertaking from the subjective mind of the individual to the shared realities of the collective, giving it the quality of **communality**. Even if we are working entirely by ourselves, we still have to relate to the world around us, including our cultural heritage, including the economic system we find ourselves in and its relative health, including our access to material and educational resources, and including the shifting tides of history just to name a few. Early humans, for example, developed language in the context of the newly emergent conscious self-awareness. Isaac Newton was able to forward his discoveries based on the previous work of other mathematicians and astronomers, most notably German astronomer and mathematician Johannes Kepler, who himself drew upon the influence of the earlier astronomical observations of Danish nobleman Tycho Brahe.

Communality touches upon the complex ecosystems of interrelatedness our species has built over the last hundred thousand years. We constantly influence and are influenced by the things around us; the context of a project unfolding in Dzang Zok, China is very different than one unfolding in Danbury, Connecticut.

This became very clear to me while working on a student design project outside of Havana, Cuba in January 2001. Because Cuba is a communist country, when we wanted various materials such as bricks, mortar, and steel, there were no hardware stores to visit or money to exchange; at every step in the process we had to petition the government, Fidel Castro's government.

For Christo and Jeanne-Claude, the communality of the project was as important as the fence itself. All the meetings and injunctions, short-comings and outbursts, all the challenges of going door to door, gathering signatures, of winning the support of one group while simultaneously inciting the anger of another, were as important to the project as the fence itself. In a recent interview with the Smithsonian, who hosted a commemorative exposition of the project, Christo said, "The fence is not the work of art. The work of art is all-togetherness."

Rarely are the shared realities of the collective a single thing; they are instead dynamic, multilayered, and often unpredictable. The local artists, for example, who shared the most in common with Christo and Jeanne-Claude turned out to be their most strident opponents. Even the fencing materials ended up having profound links to a much broader collective, an eerily significant snapshot of the state of world at that time. With the Vietnam War drawing to a close, there was a surplus of sturdy, military tent poles that had been used by the army for temporary bases during the war effort.

The fabric was another remarkable find. Apparently, on the day Christo and Jeanne-Claude called the manufacturer for prices and availability of wide panels of durable white nylon, they learned that General Motors, in the process of developing a new safety technology known as the air bag, had just rejected a large shipment of fabric that was too wide for their specifications.

The five qualities of manifestation—definability, flexibility, longevity, activeness, and communality—are the framework by which the experience of insight becomes part of our shared realities, the shared realities of our families, our communities, and our culture as well as the broader domains of art, science, and religion. Without manifestation, there is no creativity; we are left with nothing more than an ungrounded collection of great and not-so-great ideas flying about like kites whose strings have broken.

MANIFESTATION LEADING TO THE
EXPERIENCE OF INSIGHT

Over a span of 3.5 years, including 18 public hearings in two separate counties, three trips to the California Supreme Court and another to the Southern California Coastal Commission, after obtaining the signature of consent of each of the 59 land owners, and realizing the completion of a 450-page environmental impact report, the building finally began. Small crews worked for several months installing the steel poles, guy wires, and cables along the proposed route. They used helicopters, hydraulic drivers, and heavy equipment fitted with extra large floatation tires to minimize impact. The fabric was sewn and outfitted with grommets in Virginia and shipped to San Francisco in inconspicuous fruit crates designed to fool the opposition, which by that time had already sabotaged two of the artists' vehicles.

On the Labor Day weekend of 1976, 600 temporary workers were bused in from San Francisco to the Petaluma Fair Grounds, where they were trained on the raising, unfurling, and hooking of the fabric. Then, like a colony of ants, they were unleashed on the fence. The three-day weekend was chosen strategically with the idea that, should the opposition launch another appeal, it would be difficult to find a judge to stop them over the holiday.

But the opposition did not rest. As the final push was underway they countered again, appealing the validity of the permitting from the Northern California Coastal Commission. Christo and Jeanne-Claude, however, ordered the work to continue, moving all crews from Sonoma County to coastal Marin County to complete their work there before anyone could officially stop them. Christo and Jeanne-Claude even planned to abandon their headquarters and hide in the woods if need be, reasoning that the authorities would be unable to serve papers if no one could find them.

When it was completed on September 10, 1976, Running Fence had a profound effect on those who saw it. As it turned out, it was neither a fence nor a glorified laundry line, or anything that could be adequately described in words. Its presence, though clearly defined by the materials and path it traveled, was somehow ineffable and seemed to express some unspoken truth. There it was, an 18-foot-tall structure of silvery white nylon running east west across the coastal hills, the fabric from a newly emerging technology to protect the lives of motorists held in place by the remnants of the United States' most painful and dividing military campaign to date. As the sun, the wind, and the morning fog ran their fingers along the fence, so too did the zeitgeist of history, opening the hearts and minds of those who saw it.

While Running Fence seemed to have an uncanny tendency to divide people during the planning and permitting, when it was finally manifested, it became a force of unity, an undulating sail along the headlands welcoming the winds of the vast Pacific, a blank canvas chronicling the changes of day, a bridge of material stitched across the ocean and land, the manifested vision of a ribbon of light, unveiling the region's self-existing beauty.

In the documentary film, one of the ranchers is shown walking along Running Fence with a friend and, as ranchers do, testing the system by giving the lower cable a good tug. He stops at one of the poles and says to his friend, excitedly, "Try to shake this here, try to shake it. There's no way you can ever move that." He then adds, "I think I'm going to come up here and sleep here tonight. It's so nice. Sleep right here next to the fence."

Another land owner, the westernmost rancher with his property adjacent to the ocean, counts the posts marching down the hill slope, the posts and material that will be his at the end of the project. When he's done counting he says, "Beautiful!" leaving us unsure whether he's referring to the aesthetics of the fence or his own material gain. We can only imagine it is a bit of both as he says, after a long pause looking at the fabric diving into the ocean, "There's something you can hardly believe in."

Even the opposition, whose efforts became increasingly pronounced as the hearings wore on, were not immune to the effects of the fence's beauty. Years later, one Valley Ford resident who stood in opposition stated, "I sided with the majority of the people who felt that if the fence did go up, it would bring so many people into the community that it would change us. Well, it did change us. It ended up bringing people together. For the first time the local farmers and ranchers and hippies were getting together and talking about things, and often we were on the same side."

Coincidentally, one day before the fence's completion, Chairman Mao, the architect behind China's communist revolution and China's first communist leader, died, prompting a nearby Berkeley newspaper to run the headline, "Mao Dies from Jealousy." Sometime later, Christo and Jeanne-Claude received a postcard from Professor Philip Morrison from the Massachusetts Institute of Technology, a scientist who had worked on the Manhattan Project during his early years and, after surveying the devastation left after the bombing of Hiroshima, became a leading voice against nuclear proliferation. The letter contrasted the strong military boundary set by the Great Wall of China and the unifying nature of Running Fence saying, "When the Wall of China dreams, he dreams he is a Running Fence."

After 14 days, the fence was dismantled. The poles became support posts and cattle guards. The fabric became tarps and band aids for leaky barns and, in a few cases, wedding dresses for those land owners' daughters. All that remains to this day are photographs and sketches, the documentary film, the stories of those who were there, and a single pole, one of the 2,050 used in the project, now standing outside the Valley Ford post office, in service as a flag pole, a standard issue American flag in place of the ribbon of light that once was.

Christo and Jeanne-Claude would continue to lecture, raise money, and do large projects in sites around the world, including their epic 26-year journey to realize "The Gates" in Manhattan's Central Park in the winter of 2005. But Running Fence proved to be their seminal work, a remarkable achievement of size, scale, time, and effort that showed how an art installation, and a community standing both for and against it, can bring out the beauty of the land and change the hearts of the people who occupy it.

SELF-EXPRESSION:
HUSTON SMITH AND THE WORLD'S RELIGIONS

The imagination is not interested in...naively pitting one
side against another, dark against light. It is interested in
the place where the two sides meet, and what they give
birth to when they cross-fertilize each other. That is
the heart of creativity: it is not fantasy, not invention.
Creativity is listening in on the places where the
opposites are dancing with each other.

—*John O'Donohue*

One evening in the early 1920s, 65 miles northwest of Shanghai, along the banks of the Yangtze River, in the town of Dzang Zok (Changshú in Mandarin), a town surrounded by a high stone wall to protect against warlords and other terrestrial invaders, a town of intentionally winding lanes to confuse unwanted demons, a young American boy named Huston Smith, no more than a toddler at the time, was in bed with a raging fever, forming his earliest and most enduring memory, that of the precariousness of life.

Built in the Middle Ages and steeped in both age-old Taoist principles and the local folk religion, Dzang Zok was home to 100,000 inhabitants packed into a single square mile. Dzang Zok was also the location of the first Chan (Zen) Buddhist monastery in China and the home of Confucius' most beloved disciple, Yan Hui. Now, due to the efforts of Huston's missionary parents and the Christian Volunteer Movement, whose motto was "Let's Christianize the Whole World in One Generation," Dzang Zok was also home to Christianity.

AUSTIN HILL SHAW

Huston's family life, a Christian island in a sea of Eastern philosophies, was infused with Christian ideals. Driven by the desire to do God's work, and motivated by the idea that second by second souls were sinking into perdition, Huston's father worked tirelessly between the orphanage, the soup kitchen, the girls' school, and above all, the church, all of which he established upon arriving in Dzang Zok. Huston, who deeply admired his father and, in his words, "drank Christianity in with his mother's milk," set up his own parish in the family tool shed and began preaching at a young age, dreaming of one day following in his father's footsteps.

But things didn't quite turn out that way. Over the next several decades, Huston Smith would become the world's foremost authority on comparative religion, and not just as a scholar, not simply as an outsider looking in. While the religious world may have been long divided into separate and sometimes acrimonious camps, the trenchant differences between the various customs, views, and faiths the source of violent conflicts worldwide, Huston would embark on a path seldom traveled. Blessed with an insatiable curiosity and a genuine longing to get to the heart of each tradition, he would become a devotee and, to the best of his ability, an insider in many of the traditions he encountered. He would read their scriptures, consult their foremost living authorities, adopt their customs, and integrate what he could of each tradition's experiential insights, all with one driving intention in mind: to discover how "to transform our flashes of insight into abiding light."

What was it about the approach of this remarkable man that has had such a positive impact on our understanding of the world's religions? What can we learn from him to foster our own creative awakening?

INSIGHT AND MANIFESTATION TOGETHER

We have come to the third and final section on the Path of Creativity, the integration of insight and manifestation, the yoking together of two parts into a cohesive whole, yoking them together into what is paradoxically both the highest and most natural aspect of creativity, **Self-expression**. But in order to fully understand the power and significance of Self-expression, we must examine the nature of the Self, including the mechanism that allows the Self to create. In order to explore this paradoxical aspect, we will look at the life of Huston Smith and the domain of religion to see how a larger, eternal Self, which is our direct connection with the Ground of Creativity, works through our finite identity as we create. I will attempt to define this "Self" and "Self-expression" a little later on. For now, let's gather together the pieces of what we have examined so far.

We have explored the experience of insight that led the young Isaac Newton in his discovery of the Universal Law of Gravitation, a discovery that overcame the prevailing view of the day that the laws governing the heavens and the laws governing the earth had to be fundamentally different. We have also explored how the artistic expression of Christo and Jeanne-Claude led to the manifestation of a 24.5 – mile ribbon of light unifying the California coastal hills and the mighty Pacific as well as the hearts and minds of the divisive locals.

Now it is time to explore the story of an exceptional person working in the sphere of religion, a sphere that for many of us brings up strong opinions and very mixed feelings. In the context of understanding, and more importantly, *embodying* the fullest expression of creativity in our lives, and in order to understand Self-expression, it is not only important that we look at the sphere of religion, but absolutely necessary. Why? Whether our outlook is primarily secular in nature, or is punctuated with some occasional religious practice, or whether religion and spirituality are the central and most important aspect of our lives, it is nonetheless relevant. In the words of John Hale, professor of archeology at the University of Louisville, arising alongside the dawn of conscious self-awareness, "Religion occupies a primary, central place in human affairs." The world's religions are humanity's most enduring attempt to feel connected with the larger world, the quest to know the "Self" in "Self-expression."

The word "religion" comes from the same Latin root for ligaments, *ligare*, which means "to bind." Religion, then, as an *experience* is the felt sense of *rebinding*. Rebinding to what? Rebinding our full-person expression of our sensorial bodies, our agile minds, and our boundless spirits to the world around us. Moreover, as ligaments connect muscles to bones, allowing them to work *together*, our felt sense of connection with the world around us empowers us to work with it more skillfully, in a manner that is less about trying to get something to fulfill a sense of lack, but to actively participate in the miraculous unfolding of the universe.

But what on earth do religion and spirituality have to do with creativity?

In my own exploration of the creative process and in conversations with innumerable others, I have come to see how our desire to create comes from the same desire that motivates the various religions. In addition, the various religious practices—meditation, prayer, service, congregating, and ritual—all attempt to connect the individual with something larger than him or herself and, from this felt sense of connection, to guide that individual to work with others in more compassionate, more loving, more mutually beneficial ways. When we boil down creativity and religion to their most basic components, they are the same: Each strives to 1) connect with the world (insight) and 2) to engage with it in a meaningful, or, to employ a term Huston uses to describe the profundity of sacred activities, *significant* way (manifestation). No matter what we do with our time, whether we work as a photographer, physicist, programmer, or pundit, or whether we adopt the customs of a monk, missionary, or yogi, our basic human drives beyond our biological drives to survive and reproduce, are our desires to feel connected to something larger than ourselves and to affect the world around us in a meaningful way. Since their root intentions are the same, understanding the views and practices of religion can help us to better understand the views and practices guiding genuine creativity and how we can begin to live our entire lives creatively, in a state of continuous Self-expression. When we look at the life of Huston Smith we are able to observe these views and practices embodied in a genuinely creative life, a life that embodies Self-expression.

In this chapter we begin to examine the union of insight and manifestation happening in real time, and here is where the life of Huston Smith serves as a powerful example, helping us explore the fullest expression of creativity *as a way of life*. As a teacher, author, dedicated practitioner, and an exceptionally curious person, Huston Smith explored the views and adopted many of the experiential practices of the various religions he encountered, thereby coming to a deeper understanding of the sphere of religion as a whole, as well as the human and cultural conditions from which the various traditions arose. Furthermore, he was able to appreciate *both* the outward differences of various religions *and* their internal sameness. Huston adopted, and thereby experienced, each tradition's methodology for reconnecting to what I have been calling the Ground of Creativity—the dynamic, interdependent, deeply mysterious arising of this unbelievably precious world that surrounds us. Huston's life, then, serves as an example, one that can guide us in our own synthesis of insight and manifestation, a synthesis that, ultimately, enables us to embrace the power and significance of Self-expression.

Thus far in the book, I have set up the qualities of insight and the qualities of manifestation in opposition:

INSIGHT			MANIFESTATION	
Ineffability	An experience beyond words	←→	Something graspable by others	Definability
Certainty	Unshakable sense of truth in the moment	←→	Willingness to admit we might not have all the answers with time	Flexibility
Brevity	Instants, moments, hours,	←→	Hours, weeks, years, lifetimes	Longevity
Receptivity	Feeling of something coming to us	←→	Efforting to go outwards into the world	Activity
Individuality	Happening in the internal awareness of one person	←→	Happening in the shared experience of groups of people	Communality

In this way, insight and manifestation can be seen as forming a sort of polarity, an electric field of paired opposites tugging at one another from across the divide. Like the yin and yang in the Taoist tradition that leads to the ten thousand things, so, too, do insight and manifestation create the human world, the world of buildings and cityscapes, the world of art, the world of science and technology, the world of economic and political systems, and the world of religious and spiritual practices that we see all around us.

But insight and manifestation can also be seen as two irreconcilable forces that seem to be working *against* one another. How, for example, can we cultivate ineffable experiences if we are trying to clearly define the individual tasks of a project? How do we actively strive to create things in the world while still keeping ourselves open to new possibilities as time unfolds? Is it possible to wrangle the mind into diverging into the vastness of infinite potential and converging towards specifics *at the same time*?

The paradoxical nature of the Path of Creativity as expressed by its seemingly irreconcilable components—insight and manifestation—reflects the nature of reality itself. Like the tension of a guitar string drawn taut between the bridge and the nut, like the contrast between the solidity of the wood of the guitar and the emptiness of space in and around it, the paradoxes, and the tensions they create are precisely what allows the song of creation to resound, unceasingly, an unending dance of build up and release.

The world, indeed the entire universe, and our experiences of it are a play of opposites. We measure time by the difference between day and night. We understand space by the contrast between solidity and emptiness. We experience movement in relation to stillness, and love in relation to hate. Our observance of a material world sparks our curiosity about the immaterial. Our ability to grow and to learn and to know with some clarity rests on our willingness to admit our uncertainty and ignorance. And our ability to lead a genuinely creative life resides in our ability to dance in the tension between insight and manifestation. In both the creativity of the cosmos and the Path of Creativity as walked by the individual, creative potential builds in the space between paired opposites.

So how does religion work with such tension? As the Irish poet William Butler Yeats once said, "People who lean on logic, philosophy and rational exposition end by starving the best part of the mind." At present, with the powerful advances of science and technology, advances that attempt to both explain away the mysteries of the world and solve its most pressing problems, it is primarily religion that sanctifies the tension of opposites, not as something to resolve, but as a basic tenet of reality, as something to honor and celebrate. The rational mind doesn't do so well with paired opposites, but the heart, the hallowed ground of religion, does. Whether it be the distinction between heaven and earth, the relative and the absolute, samsara and nirvana, religious systems can help guide in celebrating the opposites, ultimately helping us to lead our lives in an ongoing expression of creativity, a never-ending exchange of connecting to the world and engaging with it in a meaningful way. Even Isaac Newton, whose laws and methodologies became the framework for modern science and classical physics, warned others against using them to view the universe as a mere machine. "Gravity explains the motion of the planets," he said, "but it cannot explain who set the planets in motion."

And, as we all know very well, religion is far from perfect. When religion devolves into a series of rigid beliefs its ceases to be vehicle for creativity; it ceases to allow us to abide in the space between opposites, something that we'll explore in the next chapter.

Let's see how the tension between insight and manifestation began to take shape in Huston's life, and how the play of insight and manifestation *together* leads to the possibility of what Huston referred to as "abiding light."

In 1935 Huston Smith set sail for America, crossing the Pacific and half of the North American continent, ultimately landing in the heartland of the United States, Fayette, Missouri, to attend Central Methodist College. Perhaps for many of us born and raised in the United States, Missouri might lack social or cultural interest. But for Huston, born and raised in Dzang Zok, it was a whole new frontier, exotic, fast-paced, and brimming with new possibilities.

Soon after arriving, and moved by the teachings of one of his new professors, Huston became interested in Naturalistic Theism, a branch of Christianity far different than that practiced by his parents. Naturalistic Theism argues that "all we can know for certain is this world, and religion thus consists of discovering and devoting our lives to the worthwhile in this world." Compared to the soul-saving obsession of his father, this was a grand departure indeed. Not only was Huston opening up to the world of ideas, he was no longer oriented exclusively to the Kingdom of Heaven. The manifest realm—the immediate, tangible world—was gaining importance in his mind.

In 1940, he enrolled in the University of Chicago's School of Divinity to study with the man who founded the school of Naturalistic Theism, Henry Nelson Wieman. In his time, Wieman was profoundly influential, inspiring a whole generation of Christian activists, including civil rights leader Dr. Martin Luther King, Jr. According to Huston, Wieman taught that, "God is not the creator but a creative process, superhuman but not supernatural." As Huston said, "Wieman's was an unusual understanding of Christianity, in which Christ neither reformed an old religion nor created a new one: Rather, Jesus was the catalyst that releases creative power in his disciples to transcend conventional, societal limitations." Wieman's philosophy was to do away with what he perceived as the limiting myths of Christianity, and examine the religion's deepest insights under the objective lens of science. This lens stated that all you could know was what was revealed through the senses and scientific scrutiny. This knowledge was then to be applied in creating a more just and civil society. Huston put a quote from Wieman in his billfold as a constant reminder. It read, "Faith is not belief but dedication to serving the highest goal you know."

As it turned out, Huston's love for Wieman's philosophy also led Huston to love itself. Huston married Wieman's daughter Kendra three years after he landed in Chicago, beginning a collaborative and loving relationship that has lasted over six decades.

Although Huston moved to the United States to get an education and the necessary credentials to follow in his father's footsteps, he found himself completing his Ph.D. under the influence of a professor whose immanent approach to Christianity focused on the importance of *this* world, the tangible world of the senses, using scientific objectivism to scrutinize faith-based beliefs. Huston's curiosity led him away from the understandings he grew up with into a secular branch of his beloved religion, a branch divorced from the metaphysical, a branch that was fundamentally scientific in its orientation.

Like a ballast preventing a ship from tipping too far in one direction, another heavyweight thinker entered into Huston's mind stream shortly before his graduation. That was Gerald Heard, whose book *Pain, Sex, and Time* Huston discovered while doing research for his doctoral dissertation. Once he opened the cover, he was unable to put it down. Unlike Wieman, Heard took the immediacy of the human drama occurring in the here and now—the threats posed by rampant consumerism, the possibility of ecological collapse, and the cult of the individual reigning in the West—and framed it as part of something much, much, bigger: a grand evolution, with the ever-developing human consciousness on the verge of a great break-through. Fueled by humankind's unparalleled sensitivity to pain on the one hand, and our "exaggerated capacity for sex" in compari-son to other species, which tend to be more periodic in their sexual activity, Heard argued that humankind was on the brink of what he called "the post-individualist era," in which "science and spiritual-ity will become allies, and human beings will begin to realize a vast potential, now only dimly felt.".

Furthermore, and most impactful on Huston, was "Heard's con-viction that of all the people it was the mystics, with their larger vision, who foreshadowed the mutation about to occur." Based on both his early upbringing and scholarship, Huston had known about mysti-cism all his life, that branch of religious experience concerned with the cultivation of direct and immediate spiritual truths. But despite his knowledge of such mystical experiences, he had doubts about his own capacities for divine inspiration, inspirations of the sort pro-claimed by Moses witnessing the burning bush and St. Theresa of Avila's being lifted off the ground by God's divine love. Despite his earliest memory of that feverish state when he lay on the threshold of between life and death, Huston went so far as to describe himself as "a flat-footed mystic," lacking the innate capacities to go the distance of the rapturous texts he had read throughout his early life.

Still, Huston found Heard's message incredibly captivating, and dangerously so, for he was tempted to drop out of school and adopt the age-old mystical practices, including isolation, fasting, mediation, and various forms asceticism, ultimately attempting to cultivate his own capacity for divine inspiration. Resisting this, Huston vowed not to read another word of Heard's ideas until he was done with his dissertation and had his diploma in hand, a vow which he kept.

Then, just 25 years old, with a wife and daughter and burdened by debt from graduate school, Huston was suspended between Wieman's secular message, his love for his family and need to support them and develop his career, and his mystical desire to know the love and brilliance of God firsthand. Huston found himself in a grand predicament: Was it possible to reconcile his desire for mystical union with God while fulfilling his earthly responsibilities?

For Huston, the challenges posed by the immanent Naturalistic Theism of his graduate school mentor and father-in-law and the transcendent mystical qualities of the post-individualist society presented by Gerald Heard pulled him in two different directions.

In short, Huston found himself caught between two seemingly irreconcilable opposites.

Ultimately, through a series of remarkable events, the tension would lead him to become not only the leading academic authority of comparative religion, but also an *insider*, a willing student in almost all of the religions he encountered. Be it yoga, meditation, prayer, koan practice, devotional dancing, or the ingestion of psychoactive compounds, to paraphrase an old Zen saying, not only would Huston become a preeminent authority of the different fingers pointing towards the moon, he would undertake wholeheartedly each tradition's wisdom practices for *experiencing* the moon itself.

With his roots in Christianity held firm and, simultaneously, his willingness to study and embrace the truths and practices of other religions he encountered, Huston's writing and teachings on the world's religions were far from a dry scholarly survey or academic posturing. . In the same way that Isaac Newton was able to overcome the leading idea that the laws of the heavens and the laws of the earth had to be fundamentally different, and in the same way that Christo and Jeanne-Claude were able to bridge the divide between those who were for their project and those who were against it, Huston's life began to illustrate how the tension between one's commitment to a deeply personal, internal purpose and the multifaceted demands of the world in which we live begins to loosen the boundaries between them. This blurring, if fully surrendered to, can lead to an internal experience of the world that is sacred, luminous, and deeply nourishing and an engagement with life that is interactive, empowered, and purposeful.

Upon graduation, Huston took his first teaching post at the University of Denver. Still in debt from graduate school, and with little experience to command a decent salary, money was tight. He and his family lived in a trailer home and got around on foot, bike, or bus. Still, inspired by the writing of Gerald Heard, Huston was determined to meet him face to face. He contacted Heard's publisher, conveyed his desire to meet him, then hitchhiked to Los Angeles and from there to a remote monastery where Heard was living, 70 miles to the southeast.

When Huston arrived at the monastery, he was not disappointed. The breadth and depth of Heard's knowledge, effortlessly spanning history, literature, anthropology, mythology, and the sciences, was formidable. Furthermore, Heard's underlying message deeply touched Huston, echoing the writing of the mystics, "that the world we can see and touch is not all there is." Now, after devouring Heard's writings, Huston was met with the indescribable *presence* of the man himself. Huston recalls, "After a while we sat in silence, gazing at the barren canyon walls. And the mute desert seemed to carry on our conversation for us.".

If the experience of meeting Heard wasn't enough, yet another heavyweight thinker was just around the bend. Upon leaving the monastery, Heard suggested that as long as he was in the area, Huston might want to meet a friend of his living in Los Angeles. That friend was Aldous Huxley.

Huston was elated. Born in Great Brittan and twenty-six years Huston's senior, Aldous Huxley was a formidable scholar, a celebrated writer, had a profound understanding of various religions and their practices, and, later in life, would become an advocate of the expansion of consciousness through the judicious use of psychedelic compounds. In many ways, the life led by Huxley was to foreshadow the life led by Huston.

Most impactful on Huston, Huxley was a champion of the Perennial Philosophy, a term which he popularized in his famous book by the same name, *The Perennial Philosophy: An Interpretation of the Great Mystics, East and West*. As stated by Huxley, the Perennial Philosophy has four fundamental doctrines, doctrines that would become the conceptual framework of Huston's own search for the divine:

* **First:** The phenomenal world of matter and of individualized consciousness—the world of things and animals and men and even gods—is the manifestation of a Divine Ground within which all partial realities have their being, and apart which they would be nonexistent.

* **Second:** Human beings are capable of not merely knowing *about* the Divine Ground by inference; they can also realize its existence

by a direct intuition, superior to discursive reasoning. This immediate knowledge unites the knower with that which is known.

* **Third:** Man possesses a double nature, a phenomenal ego and an eternal Self, which is the inner man, the spirit, the spark of divinity within the soul. It is possible for a man, if he so desires, to identify himself with the spirit and therefore with the Divine Ground, which is of the same or like nature with spirit.

* **Fourth:** Man's life on earth has only one end and purpose: to identify himself with his eternal Self and so to come to unitive knowledge of the Divine Ground.

Let's pause for a moment to contemplate the significance of these points in relationship to Self-expression, for herein lies our first clue into the definition of the Self. While our phenomenal ego's primary role is to insure our survival, the Self is our bridge to the universe, connecting us to that which is unborn, unchanging, unceasing. As Huxley said, it is the source from which "all partial realities have their being, and apart which they would be nonexistent". Like the sun at the center of our solar system, the Self provides us with light, heat, and stability. The capital "S" is there to remind you that this is not the same "self" that appears at the top of your check book; this is not your finite personality. The Self is what connects you with eternity.

When we are having an insightful experience, the Self is the glowing filament in the light bulb above our heads. When we are working to manifest a creative project, the Self is the fire in our hearts willing us, for some strange, unexplainable reason, to keep moving forward.

When Huston arrived at Huxley's hideout in the Mojave Desert east of Los Angeles, Huxley's book on the Perennial Philosophy, now a classic, was only in its first year of circulation. Huston on the other hand, had yet to write anything of significance and was still rooted primarily in Christianity. His time with Huxley, like an important message twice delivered, paralleled his experience with Heard. As the two of them walked in the desert that day, Huston talked of his own pursuits and his intent to move to St. Louis, to teach at Washington University that fall. Huxley, on the other hand, spoke of his love of the desert's *emptiness*, a term common to Eastern philosophies but, especially at that time, not well known and even less understood in the West, a term used to describe the web of interconnectedness behind our ordinary, superficial experience of discrete, independent things. With the cupped hands of synchronicity guiding him along, in the bold landscape of the Mojave desert, in the company of one of his heroes, it might have seemed as though Huston's experience was paralleling the journey of Christ into the desert some two millennia before, receiving just what he needed to move forward in a purposeful way.

There was more. Huxley suggested that Huston meet Swami Satprakashananda, a Vedanta Hindu practicing in St. Louis. Huston's journey into the inward path of religion was soon to depart from the confines of an exclusively Christian view. Thus, on the chance encounter of meeting Huxley through Heard, and Huxley's suggestion that he meet Swami Satprakashananda in St Louis, so too began Huston's willingness to undertake the practices of the various religions he encountered, with the ultimate intention of Huxley's Perennial Philosophy in mind, "to identify himself with his eternal Self and so to come to unitive knowledge of the Divine Ground."

Upon his arrival at Washington University in St Louis, Huston would begin his dual citizenship in earnest, one as an egoic identity going into the classroom and teaching, and one as the eternal Self, the divine spark within him stepping across the hard lines of various traditions he encountered and undertaking their practices as his own. So while he was imparting his growing knowledge at the various schools at which he taught, including Washington University from 1947 to 1958, MIT from 1958 to 1973, Syracuse University from 1974 to 1983, and UC Berkeley from 1983 to 1996, he was simultaneously diving ever deeper into wisdom itself, experiencing it through the practices of Vedanta Hinduism beginning in 1947, Zen Buddhism beginning in 1957, and the Sufi branch of Islam beginning in 1973. When Huston's oldest daughter married a Jew, his new son-in-law became Huston's link to Judaism. When Huston began visiting the Onondaga Reservation near his post at Syracuse, Chief Oren Lyons became his link to the view and customs of the primal religions.

Like a pilgrim circumambulating the base of a great mountain, with each passing decade, his mother's milk of Christianity was being enriched by these other traditions' approaches to understanding that mountain's common summit. As time progressed, he would begin each day with Hatha Yoga for his body, a passage from *Bhagavad Gita*, the *Tao Te Ching*, the *Koran*, or the good old-fashioned Methodist Bible for his mind, then pray to both enliven his spirit and to connect his practice with others. Furthermore, by adopting Islam's call to prayer five times a day for 20 consecutive years his sacred outlook spread into all parts of his day. Huston reports, "[the Islamic call to prayer] imposed rhythm and structure on my activity, which can otherwise become diffuse and scattered in all directions."

Once Huston began to internalize both the practices of the various traditions he encountered as well as furthering his understanding of religious experiences themselves, he would write on them, writing with both the discriminating awareness of a scholar and, more importantly for the animated quality he brought to each sentence, the luminous heart of a dyed-in-the-wool seeker. His now-famous book, which was first published as *Man and His Religions* in 1958, has sold over two million copies. By the time it was reworked, retitled, and rereleased in 1991 as *The World's Religions*, it included a new section on Sikhism, another on Tibetan Buddhism, which was virtually unheard of in the West before the Chinese invasion of Tibet in 1959, and one on Sufism, which by 1991, Huston had now practiced for nearly two decades as part of his practice of Islam. He also included a whole new section on the primal religions, those primarily earth-based religions that arose in the awesome wake of the dawn of conscious self-awareness. Of this last category, which Huston began to study in earnest during weekend visits to the Onondaga nation, Huston wrote, in *The World's Religions*:

> It is more than academic exercise, for we can be sure that remnants of this mode survive as psychic traits in our deep unconscious. There is also the possibility that we might learn from them, for tribes may have retained insight and virtues that urbanized, industrial civilizations have allowed to fall by the wayside.

THE INTEGRATION OF INSIGHT AND MANIFESTATION

What makes for the realization of a genuinely creative life?

A genuinely creative life holds at its core the recognition and the felt experience that the world we interact with on a daily basis and the unseen world that supports it are not two; they are one. Beyond what Aldous Huxley explained in the Perennial Philosophy, in which the primary objective of the individual is to make a relation-ship with the Divine Ground, a genuinely creative life calls us to see the Divine Ground and the phenomenal world as *inseparable*. This way of living, sometimes referred to as *nonduality*, recognizes the importance of both the Divine Ground and the phenomenal world, an approach where both divergent and convergent thinking coexist in the same moment in time.

Furthermore, as human beings with clearly demarcated corporal bodies on the one hand and boundless spirits on the other, both the experience of being human and our ability to create reside in this tension between our finite identities and our eternal Self. When we learn to reside in that place, we no longer reject some experiences in favor of others. We recognize that everything we experience–from turning a door knob, to a sense of sadness welling in our throat, to being mad at the waiter for overcharging us, to pondering our next vacation, to intuiting a cure for cancer—are all expressions of the tension of opposites, the luminous space residing between insight and manifestation, between the Divine Ground and the phenomenal world.

Simply put, the fruition of human creativity is *Self-expression*, the act of expressing the eternal Self through our finite identity, through the vessel of our body, through the portals of our hearts and minds, and the miraculous nature of our thoughts, emotions, and sensations, all of it orchestrated by the mysterious glue of conscious self-awareness. When we create, when we feel the rapture of Self-expression, we feel at home in the world; with our bodies, minds, and spirits in alignment, we revel in the experience of intimate, cosmic connectedness and active, purposeful being. We are receptive and active at one and the same time, drawing on the infinite Ground of Creativity and expressing it through our creative actions. When we create, we exhibit the fullest expression of our humanity and close the gap between heaven and earth.

When we awaken to a genuinely creative life, we begin to experience everything as sacred, worthy of reverence. Our creativity, both in the insights that come to us and our efforts to manifest those insights in the world, becomes an expression of the dynamic, interdependent, deeply mysterious world in which we live. Our creativity, including obstacles and dead ends, becomes its own expression of the universe coming into being moment after moment. As such, accepting creativity as a spiritual path can help us facilitate our felt connection to the Ground of Creativity in everything we do.

What I find most inspiring about the life of Huston Smith is the way his private life as a seeker and his public life as a teacher not only enriched his own experience as an individual, together they've lent themselves to a truly creative life, including a loving family, profound friendships with other teachers, authors, intellectuals, and religious leaders, and a long line of remarkable experiences and achievements, some made possible by his own efforts, some by the generosity of others, and some, as we will see, by the unavoidable pain and challenges of the human experience.

Perhaps the most important thing we can learn from Huston's life is this: When we are willing and courageous enough to explore what is most true and enlivening within us, it serves as both an example and an invitation, allowing others the courage and freedom to pursue their own heartfelt interests. When we honor our own lives, when we honor these incredibly complex bodies, these agile minds, and these boundless spirits, we feel the life force energy of creativity weaving together all that we do. Everything, the so-called opportunities and the so-called obstacles, all become signposts of sorts, leading us ever deeper into the dynamic, interconnected, deeply mysterious world in which we live. In other words, what begins as a hunch or inkling, or what begins in strife and anguish as a search for something "better," when fully surrendered to, reveals an incredibly vibrant, pulsating, sacred world permeating our everyday, ordinary experiences.

More specifically, when we rest in the tension between insight and manifestation, when we are able to accommodate the extremes of total absorption on one side and the identification and execution of discrete tasks on the other, a whole new set of qualities arises, qualities that get to the heart of what it means to live a truly creative life.

In the space between the ineffable and the clearly delineated, we find **imagination**. Imagination is none other than our ability to allow the habit-prone mind to relax and to play for a while in the vast space of possibility. Like waves breaking against the hard edges of the continent, we allow the ocean of infinite possibility to lap against the shoreline of practicality, creating an edge condition that teems with life and energy. In the Sufi tradition, the mystical branch of Islam, the world of imagination is symbolized by an isthmus or *barzakh,* a spit of land that connects two larger land masses. Like an isthmus, imagination has qualities of both insight and manifestation, the formless subtlety of the ineffable on one side, and the form, color, and tangibility of the clearly delineated on the other, but is something different altogether.

In the tension between certainty and flexibility, we discover **wonder**. Wonder is a type of awareness that is both open and playful, an awareness that is stimulated when all that we take to be true is suddenly delighted by the unexpected. Wonder is a potent mix of curiosity, surprise, and appreciation. Reverence, too, is often present: When we are struck by the feeling of wonder, we are tuning into the miraculous nature of the universe. Wonder requires a confidence that transcends haughty self-importance, for if we are either fearful or insecure, we won't be open to what situations are trying to show us. Wonder keeps us open to the world around us, lending itself to both the non-conceptual experience of insight and the flexibility required for creative problem solving.

Between those brief moments of insight, and the long, enduring phase of manifestation, we discover **patience**. According to Buddhism, patience is one of the essential qualities for cutting through habitual momentum and attaining realization. Patience is the learned ability to avoid reacting to situations out of frustration, irritation, anxiety, or fear. Patience undermines the obsessive need to come up with the next great idea and the frenetic need to execute it quickly, both of which are ego-driven. Instead, patience creates space for a continuous stream of insight and helps us to manifest projects without burning bridges, keeping our relationships with ourselves and others healthier over time. Without patience, the creative universe appears to unleash avalanches of obstacles. With patience, with an *embodied* acceptance of the path quality of creativity, our perception of the world becomes noticeably different, full of amazement and synchronicity.

The quality of patience, which is a way of *being* in the world, leads to a more enlivening way of *doing*, **flow**. Flow is what is found in the space between the extremes of receptivity and activeness. It is the felt sense of a regenerative energy that comes by relating with the world as it is, a way of interacting that is neither yielding nor forced. The Taoists have a name for this, *wu wei*, which means acting with-

THE SHORELINE OF WONDER

out acting or aligning oneself with the path of least resistance. When we flow, we feel energized by doing, which is very different than the feeling of depletion we sometimes have when we are fighting against the world and trying to force an outcome. Writes Lao Tzu, in the *Tao Te Ching*,

> Less and less is done
> Until non-action is achieved.
> When nothing is done, nothing is left undone.
>
> The world is ruled by letting things take their course.
> It cannot be ruled by interfering.

Finally in the tension between the individual and the collective, we cultivate our ability to **love**. Love, as defined by author and psychiatrist M. Scott Peck is "the will to extend one's self for the purposes of nurturing one's own or another's spiritual growth." According to Huston, the historic Jesus, for example, chose love, which brought people together, over holiness, the need to designate what is pure and what is not or to divide people into "the chosen" or "the damned."

When we commit to leading a creative life, our love and appreciation for others grows. We begin to resonate with the way the insights of all the individuals throughout time have contributed to the world we see today. The language we use, the clothing we wear, the houses in which we live, even the ideas we find important, all originated from someone else's mind, all originated from their willingness to bring their own insights to fruition. Furthermore, when we recognize this, when we recognize and acknowledge the contributions of others, abundance and generosity come naturally. When we "give" in the spirit of love, we aren't left with a sense of giving something up, but with something far more basic: Every creative act re-affirms our deeply intimate, interdependent relationship with the world in which we live. As expressed by Isaac Newton, "If I have seen a little further it is by standing on the shoulders of giants."

INSIGHT		SELF-EXPRESSION	MANIFESTATION	
Ineffability	An experience beyond words	Imagination The isthmus between the known and unknown worlds something graspable by others	Something graspable by others	Definability
Certainty	Unshakable sense of truth in the moment	Wonder Awareness beyond self-importance	Willingness to admit we might not have all the answers with time	Flexibility
Brevity	Instants, moments, hours,	Patience Creating space for continuous insight and gradual manifestation	Hours, weeks, years, lifetimes	Longevity
Receptivity	Feeling of something coming to us	Flow Effortless Action	Efforting to go outwards into the world	Activeness
Individuality	Happening in the internal awareness of one person	Love Extending oneself for the sake of spiritual growth	Happening in the shared experience of groups of people	Communality

In all of these realms, Huston Smith has led a remarkably creative life. He has walked the Path of Creativity for his own benefit—deepening his personal relationship with the Absolute—and to benefit others, by sharing those insights through teaching, writing, and by throwing himself into the most pressing issues of his time. He has established friendships with religious leaders Thomas Merton, the Dalai

Lama, the legendary Islamic writer Seyyed Hossein Nasr, and Chief Oren Lyons; intellects Aldous Huxley, Gerald Heard, and Joseph Campbell; scientists Werner Heisenberg and Robert Oppenheimer; social catalyst and civil rights leader Dr. Martin Luther King, Jr., and modern trickster and renegade Harvard psychologist turned LSD messiah Timothy Leary. And he had been present at historical events as diverse as the inauguration of the United Nations and the student protests in China's Tiananmen Square.

Between the cultivation of his ineffable relationship to the Absolute and his lifelong career as a scholar, author, and teacher, Huston's life has been full of imagination. One only needs to pick up one of his many books to know his understanding of the world's religions wasn't exclusively academic. Like the animated qualities of celebrated wisdom texts, Huston's words leap from the page. They are beautifully written, adorned with lively metaphors and analogies, and reflect the living qualities of each tradition he encounters. For example, in his exploration of Hinduism's view on the challenges of the human condition, Huston writes, "No more capable of seeing our total selves in perspective than a three-year-old who has dropped its ice cream cone, our attention is fixated on our present life span. If we could mature completely we would see that lifespan in a larger setting, one that is, actually, unending."

In another example, one arguing for the importance of religion in the age of information, as it relates to living a genuinely creative life, Huston wrote, "The larger the island of knowledge, the longer the shoreline of wonder." Finally, on comparative religion in general Huston writes, "If we lay aside our preconceptions about these religions, seeing each as forged by people who were struggling to see something that would give help and meaning to their lives; and if we then try without prejudice to see ourselves what they saw—if we do these things, the veil that separates us from them can turn to gauze." Where others have erected walls and barriers between the various traditions, emphatically focusing on their irreconcilable differences, Huston's imagination has been timely and unique, celebrating their differences while drawing an even bigger circle around all that comprises their common ground.

Whereas the contemporary world has put the validity and importance of religion in the background of dazzling advances in the realm of science and technology, Huston returns us to the various traditions' take on the ultimate nature of reality, unveiling the alive and animated universe beyond the blinders of scientific reductionism. "The worthful aspects of reality—its values, meaning, and purpose," writes Huston, "slip through the devices of science in the way that the sea slips through the nets of fishermen."

In the middle ground between his heartfelt truths and the multifarious beliefs and opinions of others, Huston's sense of wonder also flourished. His dedication to get to the heart of the truths of the various traditions and adopt the particular flavor of their practices as his own ultimately led him to a rare, precious, and embodied understanding of the living roots of human culture. Like a linguist fluent in several languages, Huston's dedication to the Divine through a variety of means allowed him to communicate an understanding of religion and its value that is unprecedented in its breadth, depth, and inclusivity.

Furthermore, Huston's goal in teaching was never to appear academically superior to his students. He wanted there to be genuine understanding and new insights for everyone in the lecture hall, including himself, which meant remaining curious about his students' experiences and their interpretations of his teachings. His wonder also expressed itself in his willingness to try new things. When National Education Television (NET), the forerunner of the Public Broadcasting System, asked him to teach his university course "The Religions of Man" on the air in 1955, the program director, Mayo Simon, told Huston, "Lose a TV attention for 30 seconds and you're dead." Huston listened and did his best to remove excessive jargon, making his presentations alive and accessible to his new audience of 100,000. He also credits the short attention span of television viewers for both the popularity of his written work and his ability to teach.

Huston's patience is evident in his ability to complete something as grand and overarching as *Man and His Religions,* then, based on his ever-deepening intimacy with the material itself, add significant portions to the book over the years. His daily practices—yoga, contemplative study, meditation, and prayer—contributed significantly to his patience, activating awareness across the full spectrum of his body, mind, and spirit, consistently refreshing and reframing his day in the sacred. When he began the Islamic call to prayer five times a day, he expanded the practice of touching in with the Absolute throughout the day in order to diffuse the headiness and self-importance that can sometimes accompany academic work and writing.

As for flow, Huston's embodied presence through his dedication to his practices and his service to others created not only a sense of flow in his own life, but one that has inspired and motivated others. For example, it occurred to one of the fans of his television program, William H. Danforth, head of Ralston Purina, that Huston hadn't actually been to most of the places he taught about. In a letter to Huston, Danforth wrote:

*If the university would grant you a semester's leave and you added
your summer vacation to it, a check to fund a round-the-world trip
for you and your wife will be in the mail.*

Huston jumped at the offer, and spent his days delving into the
cultural practices of the places he visited and traveling by night to
save both money and time, drinking in the power of ritual and religion in their places of origin. Huston writes:

> I trained with Zen roshis in Japan, in India I practiced yoga
> with Hindu yogis. I whirled with the whirling dervishes in Iran.
> In Mexico I sweated in sweat lodges and took peyote with the
> Huicholes. I meditated with Buddhist monks in Burma, I camped
> with Aborigines in Australia. I made a pilgrimage to Mount Athos,
> the Holy Mountain in Greece. At a holy festival on the subconti-
> nent among the millions of devotees and naked sadhus I wore only
> a dhorti under that blazing sun. I have taught innumerable stu-
> dents about world religions, but my teacher of the world's religions
> was the world.

Finally, in the space between the individual and the collective,
Huston practiced love, consciously opening up his heart to include
wider and wider spheres of interest, which, despite Huston's natural
warmth and enthusiasm, wasn't always easy.

When Huston arrived at Washington University in St. Louis, for
example, the school was segregated. So he invited civil rights leader
Martin Luther King, Jr. to lecture at the school. A year later, the
school dropped its racist policy. Says Huston, "The great changes
in history occur, I believe, not through argument but through seeing
things differently."

When he was asked to head the prestigious Massachusetts Institute
of Technology's new philosophy department, Huston's heartfelt,

humanistic approach to understanding religion was ridiculed by his analytic colleagues, leaving him feeling isolated and depressed. "My popularity among undergraduate students was taken by my colleagues as proof that I must be an inferior philosopher indeed." But instead of allowing it to make him bitter, he deepened his sympathies for those against whom society had "stacked the odds."

His lifelong partnership with his wife, Kendra, his love of his children and grandchildren, as well as their personal family losses, are the most telling of his dedication to love. When their oldest daughter, Karen, was nearing her fiftieth birthday, she was diagnosed with a rare and aggressive form of sarcoma cancer. She died shortly thereafter. Not long after, Huston's granddaughter Serena, enchantingly beautiful both inside and out, was murdered, leaving, he says, "a hole in life that could never be filled."

Such grave and tragic losses could easily push another to give up on the world and to retreat into bitterness. And for a time, especially after the death of Serena, Huston did retreat into a dark room, alone and inconsolable. But in their absence, he returned to all that he'd practiced, using his losses to deepen both his awareness and his compassion for the losses of others. Returning again to the wisdom teachings, he wrote, "The fact that all the things we hold dear and love are transient does not mean that we should love them less but—as I do Karen and Serena—love them even more. Suffering, the Buddha said, if it does not diminish love, will transport you to the farther shore."

Drawing upon the life of Huston Smith, the perennial philosophers, and the wisdom of the traditions, a genuinely creative life is not something we do now and then or here but not there, nor is a genuinely creative life something we do exclusively in one of the realms of art, science, and religion, to the exclusion of the others. As every chef is also a chemist, as every materials engineer must intuit a hypothesis to test, and as every renunciate must have a body and desires to renounce, a genuinely creative life is an expression of the totality of our experience, our finite lives, and all that has created them intersecting the infinite contributions of others, including the astounding creations of nature, the cosmos, and all the unknowable contributions of the unseen worlds.

My Encounter with Huston Smith

On a gloomy day in early November, 2009, I went to interview Huston Smith in the Berkshire Assisted Living center, on Sacramento Street in southwest Berkeley. Arriving by bike and bundled up against the autumn chill, the temperature in the building felt stiflingly warm. I quickly removed layers so as not to arrive at Huston's door sweating.

Though I'd never been there before, the place felt familiar. It reminded me of where my beloved grandmother lived during the last several years of her life. Like Huston, she too had left her faith from birth and joined another when she married my grandfather. But her journey was far more localized: she gave up her Southern Baptist roots to become a Methodist, under the familiar umbrella of Texas-style Protestantism. When I took refuge in Vajrayana Buddhism, she felt more than a bit worried about the state of my soul. But after four days spent at her assisted living center, and a discriminating reading of Vietnamese Buddhist monk Thich Nhat Han's book, *Living Buddha, Living Christ*, she felt more comfortable and even supportive of my decision.

I knocked on Huston's door and he called me in. I walked through a narrow hallway to an open area at the end where I found Huston near a window, curtains drawn, with a twin bed on one side, a desk on the other, and two chairs at ninety degrees to one another, one for me and the other for him. A bookcase, mostly empty, stood between the desk and Huston's chair. "I'm leaving this facility the week before Thanksgiving," he told me, "I mention that because I don't have my library here, my library is at home." There was something offsetting about seeing that near-empty bookshelf adjacent to this man I so admired, Huston Smith, author of *The World's Religions*. It was as though my own desire to finish my book and my superficial acceptance of impermanence were being by the scene in front of me.

The anticipation of spending time with a true hero of mine had me feeling both excited and nervous. I'd labored over a set of questions to ask him, and, knowing that Huston was hard of hearing, I printed the questions up ahead of time using extra large font. Being an architectural designer, and wanting to root the discussion in my so-called area of expertise, my questions to Huston on that day were centered around the links between religion, spirituality, and design. Though I felt somewhat confident when I drafted my questions, my own understanding of the subject matter seemed quickly to unravel in Huston's presence.

I began by asking Huston to speak on the similarities and differences between spirituality and religion.

"Do you recognize the name Monica Lewinsky?" Huston asked.

"Yes," I replied

"*Sixty Minutes* asked Monica Lewinsky, 'President Clinton confessed that he sinned. Do you think you sinned?' And Lewinsky said, 'Well, I'm not very religious. I'm more spiritual.'"

We both burst into laughter, with Huston clarifying that spirituality, especially in its contemporary context, was a sort of "do-it-yourself religion" in which you can fill in whatever you want.

Next I asked, "What has been the importance of religion and religious/spiritual practices in the evolution of humankind?"

"I will begin with the ending first." And referring to the book *Ritual and Religion in the Making of Humanity* by Roy Rappaport, Huston replied, "If there are going to be further developments they will be in the way of ritual and religion."

He then went on to say, "Now, I'm going to throw in a curve here on the 'evolution of humankind.' I think it will be worthwhile for me to step to my desk and bring you a page of what I have writen that bears upon this. Just relax. Loaf your soul." Huston, who once stood well over six feet tall, labored up out of his chair and, now hunched by osteoporosis and several inches below my 5' 9" frame, shuffled over to his desk. There he methodically searched for a file on his computer, printed out a page he had recently written and handed it to me. I read it as he slowly made his way back to his chair. In it, he noted that the word "'evolution,'… has slipped into the modern mind on the coattails of 'progress'."

I quickly glanced down at my list of questions, and, growing increasingly mortified, saw that I had used the phrase "evolution of humankind" throughout my list.

We trudged on.

"What is the importance, if any, of traditional religious/spiritual practices such as meditation, yoga, prayer, and assembly in the post-modern world?" I asked

Huston replied, "The key word here is 'post-modern.' How do *you* define post-modern?"

I flubbed out an answer, referring to it as " the degenerative phase of the modern," knowing well that despite having batted around the term 'post-modernity' in both my studies as an architecture student and in my time with the Buddhist community, I didn't *really* know what I was talking about. The words and their meaning weren't integrated in my full understanding of them.

Huston graciously responded, "That's not bad. Yours characterizes the quality of degeneration. But I think a more standard definition of post-modern is there are no absolutes." Then, in answer to my question he said, "The practices of meditation, yoga, and prayer are perennial. They have their place in whatever is going on chronologically. They are not determined by where or by when. Prayer is not time specific, say Third Century BC. People pray all over the world all the time. They are important, and they are constantly important. But they are not governed by when and where."

After about an hour, he said that it was time to go. I thanked him, gathered my things, and headed back out into the slate-grey day, feeling bewildered and more than a little embarrassed by my lack of understanding of my own subject matter.

In time, though, my sense of unrest over my interview with Huston revealed itself as an opening; it eventually led me to a sense of something far more fundamental, far more grounded than design, and that was creativity itself. What I would ultimately take away from my interview with Huston Smith is this: While the drive to design inspires some humans, the desire to create, to connect with the world and affect it in a meaningful way, is universal.

Since that day, I have gone back and listened to our interview several times and what stands out is this: At the end of the interview, in answer to my question, "What ideas, attitudes and/or feelings should be at the forefront of a designer's mind when beginning a design project?"

Huston replied, "Anything that we can do to enhance the beauty—visual beauty in the light, and love as the beauty in human relationships—anything that we can do in that direction is of an inestimable value to the world."

PART THREE

FRUITION

PUTTING IT ALL TOGETHER:
THE LIGHT BOX AT PRANA DEL MAR

There is a vitality, a life force, an energy, a quickening that is
translated through you into action, and because there is only one
of you in all of time, this expression is unique. And if you block it,
it will never exist through any other medium and it will be lost.
The world will not have it. It is not your business to determine
how good it is or how valuable nor how it compares with other
expressions. It is your business to keep it yours clearly and
directly, to the keep the channel open.

—*Martha Graham*

In the fall of 2010, a friend of mine named Erik Singer was struggling to make his newly opened health and wellness center in Baja,
California, Prana del Mar, profitable. Nearly seven years earlier, in
the winter of 2004, he had been struck by a moment of insight, conceived of a plan, and began looking for land. In early 2005, he hired
an architect, an engineer, and a contractor, and began constructing
his first building, the Casita, a residence and garage with an open-air
practice space covered by a prominent palapa roof.

Over the next four years Erik went on to build a 512-square-
meter (5500-square-foot) Community Building with a 94-square-
meter (1010-square-foot) rooftop deck, a prominent pool deck with
a spa, lap pool, wet deck, and sculptural outdoor shower, and eight
condominium units with a total of 32 beds. He built wandering
pathways, set up a labyrinth, dug a 20-meter well, trucked in pro-
pane tanks, placed solar panels on all the roof tops and erected solar
hot water systems for the pool, planted an organic garden to provide

fresh greens for cooking, and engineered a massive flood control embankment that ran half the long length of his property to ward of seasonal hurricane deluges. Not only that, he had to learn the language, understand the unique customs of the locals, and navigate a complex and sometimes intimidating bureaucracy, weaving through an almost overwhelming tangle of regulations stemming from various governing agencies.

When Prana Del Mar opened, in late 2009, guests and visiting health instructors alike raved about the beauty of the landscape, the friendliness of Erik's staff, the spaciousness of their accommodations, the quality of the meals, and the harmonious tranquility of his facility as a whole.

But Erik's timing could not have been worse. As the world economy was grinding to a halt and news of the violent Mexican drug wars were ramping up, much of his potential client base elected to stay north of the border, either unable or unwilling to make the trip south, all of which affected me deeply.

Not only was I Erik's friend, I was also the project's architect.

We'll be looking at the evolution of this project to illustrate the themes of creativity explored throughout this book.

Thus far we have explored the lives of some remarkable and influential figures in their domains, including Isaac Newton from the domain of science, Christo and Jeanne-Claude from the domain of art, and Huston Smith from the domain of religion, all of whom have received considerable attention for their work. Over the course of these final chapters, I have two intentions.

My first intent is to take all that we have learned about creativity thus far and present two complimentary summations, expressed as "Putting It All Together" and "Pulling It All Apart."

In this first chapter, "Putting It All Together," I will use Erik's and my experience of developing a small building on the grounds of Prana del Mar to underscore the broader mechanics of creativity, exploring the relationships between insight, manifestation, and Self-expression. I will also demonstrate creativity's ties to the three main ways in which we engage the world—through our bodies, our minds, and our spirits—and I will explore creativity's links to the three principle domains of distinctly human activities, specifically science, art, and religion. My hope is that in reading this chapter, you will be left with an intimate understanding of both the larger view of creativity and its mechanics, ultimately helping you to understand where and when to apply certain time-tested techniques from each of those domains to foster your own creativity.[4]

The next and final chapter, "Pulling It All Apart," will focus more on the *internal* journey of creativity, the sometimes joyful, sometimes painful process of undoing the knots of our own habitual patterns so that we can be more available to the world and truly take our place as *creators*. Since I know my own life more intimately than I do anyone else's, I will be using another one of my creative journeys, my most profound and challenging creative journey to date, to illustrate what I'm talking about.

My second intent is to *make these ideas personal*, to demonstrate how these lessons on creativity are not only applicable to game changers like Isaac Newton, Christo and Jeanne-Claude, and Huston Smith, or for that matter Steve Job, Emily Dickinson, and Frank Gehry, but to you. Since every one of us has arisen from a wildly creative, interdependent universe, and each of us is endowed

---

[4] I go into more depth about applying specific techniques to the process of creativity in my follow-up book, *Further along the Shoreline of Wonder: How to Live a Creative Life*.

with conscious self-awareness and all the remarkable traits that go with it, I want to infuse every fiber and every cell of your body with this simple fact: Creativity is your natural state. Have you ever wondered, for example, why it feels so good to find yourself in the creative flow? It's because you're returning home to your most fundamental expression of your humanity. Simply put, as a human, you are a creator.

So, let's return for a moment to my basic definition of human-centric creativity: 1) to connect with the world and 2) to affect it in a meaningful way. Connecting with the world involves transcending habit and experiencing life in a way that is fresh and enlivening, making way for what I call *the experience of insight*. Affecting the world in a meaningful way involves taking the experience of insight and translating it in a way that can be shared with others, what I call *manifestation*. When insight and manifestation are combined, we discover Self-expression and some of the most celebrated aspects of the human experience—imagination, wonder, patience, flow, and love. Together the passive experience of insight, the active effort of manifestation, and the five qualities of Self-expression lead individuals and organizations to bring new and enlivening creations into the world.

Finally, in any successful creative project, all of the qualities of the Ground of Creativity—luminous dynamism, miraculous interplay, and mysterious complexity—are apparent in some way. And by exploring how those qualities come into being, by exploring the path as walked by the individuals involved, we can trace what arises spontaneously, what is solved through effort, and where the qualities of imagination, wonder, patience, flow, and love play themselves out.

Origins of Prana Del Mar

Erik's initial insight to develop and run his own wellness center can be traced back to an experience he had at a retreat hosted by his younger sister in a remote location in Argentina. During that week, a facilitator led ten participants in a regimented practice of yoga, meditation, journaling, and the setting and revisiting of intentions.

Toward the end of the retreat Erik remembered walking by a mirror, stopping, and staring at his image. As he recalls, "What I was looking at wasn't me." It was as though he was no longer limited by the confines of his finite identity. "It wasn't intellectual, just something I felt."

And he felt it deeply. The experience was indescribably liberating. He'd heard others talk of such profound personal epiphanies before. But this marked an important opening in Erik's own perception of the world.

Though intelligent, well-read, and articulate, and having attended the workshops of numerous spiritual teachers, Erik didn't see himself as a spiritual teacher. But he did see his potential as spiritual host. He did see an opportunity to set a stage where others could have such openings, "where," as he told me recently, "people could have an *ah-ha* moment, have an epiphany, be opened to a part of themselves that in all their seeking they'd only understood intellectually." Erik wanted to set a stage for an experience "that transcended, or more profoundly, circumvented that whole mental process, like a bell reverberating around you." And so he began searching for a place to manifest his insight, to become both the set designer and stagehand creating the setting for his participants to have their own experiential insights.

Having spent much of his childhood in the high desert of Santa Fe, and having fallen in love with the ocean during surf trips to Baja, he settled on a remote plot of land halfway between Cabo San Lucas and Todo Santos, a place know as Migriños, several kilometers from any services. With the Sierra de Laguna Mountains rising 4000 feet above sea level to the east, the amazing allure of the cobalt blue ocean to the west, and the surreal contrast between the dryness of the land so close to the water, he felt at home. He set up a tent and an ammo can for a toilet and began the long journey of designing and building a retreat center geared toward health and wellness.

Though abundant in natural beauty, the site had some significant challenges. The property was long in the direction perpendicular to the ocean, and significantly shorter in the other.

Arroyos flanked two sides of the property, arroyos that were prone to flooding during the seasonal hurricanes. A large sand dune adjacent to the ocean did its best to block ground level ocean views on the west end. Even though its location right along the Tropic of Cancer kept the temperature fairly mild, the dryness of the desert itself caused wild temperature swings throughout the day and night. Since many of the sought-after activities, most notably yoga, were practiced just after sunrise, and since most yogis like their yoga rooms unusually warm, this would prove to be a significant challenge. The site was entirely off the grid, meaning that all the heating, cooling, and electricity would have to be produced on site or brought in from a distance.

Though I was still relatively inexperienced as a designer, my role as the architect for the project was a natural choice. I'd known Erik since 1988. We were housemates for a year in North Berkeley, he a recent Stanford graduate and myself a sophomore at UC Berkeley.

Having participated in student-based service learning design projects in Havana, Cuba, and Cuernavaca, Mexico in 2001, and having worked in an architectural studio in Bilbao, Spain in 2003, I was familiar with the culture, fluent in the language, and had experience with local building methods. In the fall of 2004, Erik flew me down to Mexico first as an adviser; after he built the Casita as a test with a local architect, he hired me to design the rest of the facility. From 2005 to 2009, communicating primarily by email, the two of us, along with a local contractor and engineer named Antonio Manriquez, for whom this was also the largest project of his career, designed the Community Building, the pool deck, the condominium units, and then reworked the Casita to solve some practical issues and aesthetically blend the old with the new.

CREATIVITY ACROSS SCIENCE, ART, AND RELIGION

There are innumerable ways in which we engage the world around us. But if we step back a bit, we begin to notice three basic ways of engagement using 1) our bodies 2) our minds and 3) our spirits. (In my own exploration, emotions don't fit into any one category nor can they be entirely placed on their own. Their variety and complexity seem to play themselves out at all levels, with our basic sense of desire or revulsion acting at the bodily level, more complex emotions such as concern, pride, and jealousy occurring at the mental level, and more expansive feelings of peace, compassion, and the felt sense of truth occurring at the level of spirit).

In reality, our bodies, minds, and spirits engage the world concurrently. We often notice one of them as dominant in any given situation, however. For example, when we are eating or exercising, we are engaging the world in a primarily bodily/sensorial manner. When we are taking an exam or mulling something over in our head, or even when we are in conversation with another, we are primarily using our thoughts. When we experience ecstasy or trauma, or when we are at the frontiers of existence, witnessing the birth of a child or the death of a loved one, our experience tends to be more spiritual.

No coincidence, there are also three principle domains of uniquely human activities—science, art, and religion. Science, the youngest of the three domains, primarily engages the sensorial world, creating first a hypothesis then testing it through a carefully constructed experiment that can be repeated by others. On the outside, science may be seen as a mental pursuit. But at its core, it relies primarily upon our ability to measure and test, which means that it must take place in the sensorial world, or as we described earlier, the *manifest realm*. Those phenomena that cannot be measured, quantified, or empirically tested fall outside the realm of science.

Science is one of the most advanced systems we have available for describing the physical world around us and putting it to use. By studying the world using the scientific method, and by putting such discoveries to work through applied sciences such as chemistry, engineering, and allopathic (Western) medicine, human beings have reduced drudgery, increased the variety of experience available to any one person, built infinitely complex cities and transportation systems, identified and fought disease-bearing micro-organisms, and more than doubled the average life span.

In contrast, religion is concerned with helping us get beyond our thoughts and beyond an exclusively sensorial, exclusively material experience of the world and to connect those experiences to something much larger. Preceding both art and science by some 100,000 years, religion is concerned with helping us to experience the ongoing interdependence of the universe that makes everything possible. At its best, religion consists of the tools and techniques humans have developed over tens of thousands of years to rise beyond the confines of their own bodies and minds and experience the abiding light, the self-existing wholeness and relatedness that underlies everything.

Between science and religion, we find art, which, so far as archeologists can tell, emerged some 30,000 years ago. Art, or more specifically, an artistic approach to life is at the core of Self-expression. It expresses the paradox of our individuality meeting our inherent connectedness to the world, our eternal Self shining through our finite ego's actions. Art mediates between the objective observations of science and the subjective inner experience explored by religious practices, bringing the inner experience into outer form. In any work of art we get a glimpse of 1) the person who made the art as well as 2) the evidence of that person engaging the world around them. Picasso, for example, pushed paint around canvases. Shakespeare performed alchemy with words. Duchamp is best known for his thought experiments: He placed a standard issue urinal on its side in a gallery, thereby questioning the nature of art itself. By first having some insightful experience, then translating that experience into form or exploring the insightful experience in the material itself, not only did their art express a message to others, it expressed the artists' *personalities*, their own unique lens on the world. Ultimately, art links both the sensorial and spiritual worlds by creating something that delights us or provokes us in some way. Art that moves us does so by allowing others to experience the world in a more profound or unexpected way.

All of human creativity has elements of art, science, and religion. Let's take a further look.

The experience of insight, that spark of creativity that initiates the whole process, could best be described as a "religious" experience. My own definition of the qualities of insight—ineffability, certainty, brevity, and passivity—are based on the writings of one of the pioneers of both religious studies and modern psychology, William James. His chapter on mysticism in his profoundly influential book, *The Varieties of Religious Experience*, illuminated the essence of insightful experiences for me. The practices developed by the mystics, including such age-old activities as meditation, fasting, prayer, and vision quests, represent some of humanity's most powerful technologies, technologies that can help us both explore the universe within us and cultivate a felt sense of our interdependence with all things, a felt sense that leaves us open to the experience of insight.

The objective nature of manifestation corresponds with the scientific outlook: It allows us to evaluate what we are doing as we go along, and adapt our creative undertakings to the laws of nature. The scientific mindset also allows us to step back and *objectively* observe what we are doing, which can help us to clarify which ideas to pursue and which to abandon.

Finally, the artistic quality of creation involves the finite individual intersecting eternity. Something that is done artfully delights the senses, nourishes the intellect, and points to something ineffable *all at the same time*. In other words, art, like imagination, serves as a bridge between the objective world of science (and the delighting of both our senses and sensibilities) and the ineffable world of the spirit. Drawing on the best of both worlds, art allows the external expression of beauty to guide us deeper into the inward experience of virtue.

The opposites are also true: The failures of science, art, and religion result when they cease to be truly *creative* endeavors. In other words, they fail when they stop 1) connecting with the world or 2) affecting the world in a meaningful way or 3) both. Science fails when it stops actually observing the world and becomes a vehicle or mouthpiece for special interest groups. In this way, science stops being an ever-evolving source of knowledge and degrades into weaponry; it becomes a battering ram for selling bogus products ("scientifically proven to reduce stress!") or, in its more defensive stance, becomes a way of avoiding responsibility, as in, "you can't prove it (scientifically) therefore I'm not responsible." Science also falls short when it denounces all that can't be quantified or measured as being nonexistent. Science also fails when it degrades into "scientism," the fanatic notion that science is the most authoritative of the three domains and not simply an important *component* of human creativity.

Religion faces similar challenges when it ceases being creative. Religion excels in offering sets of practices such as prayer, meditation, vision quests, rituals, and fasting that allow individuals glimpses of a deeper reality beyond the noise of discursive thinking and reason. When we get beyond such thought noise, we are left with the fertile field of unbridled creative potential. Religion, however, becomes toxic when it proclaims such subjective truths as "the only truths" and then *imposes* them on others. This sort of religious activity involves the reduction of the *experience* of absolute truths, which is also the experience of insight, into rigid belief systems that are used to control others. Religion also fails when it blacklists natural biological drives such as sex, or emotions such as jealousy, or uses its teachings to oppress its own members or to castigate other groups. And like science, religion fails when it stops being a good neighbor and sees itself as the most important of the three domains.

Perhaps less controversial than science and religion, art can offend us when it is poorly executed (scientific), uninspired (religion), or both. Think of a living room that seems cramped or impersonally spacious, or a packaging label where the colors seem to clash, or a toaster that looks perfect on your countertop but incinerates your muffins. In all of these, the overall creativity, either the insight or the manifestation, or the combination of the two, is somehow lacking.

But when we get it right, there's definitely a sense of magic. The whole of our progression as a species, including all the verifiable discoveries and technological advances, all the knowledge we've accumulated and stories we've gathered, and all the rituals and practices we've come up with to expand our awareness beyond ourselves, are about getting it right. Through the lens of science, creativity is the infinite number of moments that have transformed the pin prick of infinitely small, infinitely dense matter into the universe we observe today. Through the lens of art, creativity is the willingness of the artist to engage the qualities of his or her materials and the nuances of the human experience and combine them in ways that shed new light on both. And through the lens of religion, creativity is simply our deepest longing to connect with something greater than ourselves and affect the world in a positive way.

Here's a summation:

INDIVIDUAL	CREATIVITY	COLLECTIVE
SPIRIT	INSIGHT	RELIGION
MIND	SELF-EXPRESSION	ART
BODY	MANIFESTATION	SCIENCE

BIRTH OF AN INSIGHT

Let's explore how the individual experience of body, mind, and spirit and the collective domains of science, art, and religion began to play themselves out in the developments at Prana del Mar.

Whereas Erik's initial desire to develop Prana del Mar was sparked by his own profound experience of insight (religious experience), his ability to develop it over the next five years (scientific objectivism) was based on being able to accurately assess his resources, to plan, and to execute his plan. And while his opening season brought rave reviews from the teachers and guests who came (their felt sense of Self-expression), he had to do something to increase his revenues if the center was to survive in the long run (financial reality).

Erik began assessing the situation. The first thing he noticed was this: Even though Prana del Mar had a maximum occupancy of 32 guests, most groups showed up with no more than 16 people. Furthermore, some of the teachers and retreat leaders who contracted with Prana del Mar were facing the same dire economy, and would cancel at the last minute, leaving Prana del Mar with no revenues whatsoever and idle staff to pay.

If Erik could book two or more groups at a time he could increase revenues and decrease the likelihood of slow weeks. But since most groups came for specific health-related programs and wanted space for both teachings and practices, it became obvious that the practice studio atop the Casita was insufficient.

Secondly, Erik recognized that he could also improve his situation by adding more treatment rooms for his guests, thereby giving them more options to feel nourished and revitalized and generating more revenue for Prana del Mar. We'd already placed two treatment rooms on the lower level of the Community Building. But those, too, were a bottle neck, because most guests didn't want treatments right after meals, or too close to exercising nor too early or late in the day.

After weathering four years of construction and five hurricane seasons, run himself ragged providing the needed paperwork to the various government organizations, and been burned several times by subcontractors, , Erik was nonetheless determined to make things work. He contacted me in March of 2011 to explore the possibility of adding another practice studio and some treatment rooms. "I'm a bit crazed here, but hanging in there," he wrote. Then, half-jokingly he added, "If this business doesn't kill me, then Mexico surely will."

With that, we got to work again, masterminding a new building with the goal of making his retreat center financially solvent.

When we began designing the new building we'd already established an inviting material palette. Erik and I both loved Mexican architecture, but very different styles. He was drawn to the clean, sometimes austere aesthetic of the Spanish mission style, monolithic white walls contrasted with heavy dark wood. I was drawn to the more modern and celebratory designs of Pritzker Prize-winning architect Luis Barragán, who brought the raucous liveliness of the pre-colonial markets—blues, greens, yellows, and pinks—into his celebrated projects. Barragán's home in Mexico City and his remarkable convent, *La Capilla de Las Capuchinas*, profoundly impacted me when I toured them in 2001.

Combining our two tastes, the buildings we designed were primarily rectilinear, constructed with concrete blocks, the material of choice in Mexico, covered with rough white stucco. We balanced these predominantly masculine forms with more feminine ones, rough hewed beams and columns, curving balcony railings, rounded planters, and massive ceramic pots. The hardy branches of *palo de arco,* a local plant, lay across the beams of the shading devices to create a beautiful, filtered light. We also used red *pulido* floors, a local way of adding color to wet concrete, as well as black river stone insets to add patterns and texture. Bamboo flooring was used in the practice studio. In order to keep visitors connected with the wildly beautiful landscape, we devised a pocketing door system in the Community Building and condominiums and put in large windows in the practice room atop the Casita. As visitors moved throughout the buildings, they were in constant visual contact with the mountains, the desert, and the vast blue ocean.

We had also established the rigorous use of the golden rectangle, a proportioning system ubiquitous in art, architecture, and natural systems. When I was an architecture student, the idea of proportions—the way in which the dimensions of a space feel either harmonious or dissonant—baffled me. Two years after graduating, however, while designing a shrine room for my Buddhist teacher, I came across *The Power of Limits,* by György Doczi, a book dedicated to the golden rectangle. Though it sat in the architecture section of the bookstore, what caught my eye was the same familiar logo as the dharma books I'd been devouring, Shambhala Publications. I opened up the first page to read, "The discipline inherent in the proportions and patterns of natural phenomena, and manifest in the most ageless and harmonious works of man, are evidence of the relatedness of all things." *POW!* I purchased the book, and began to study its fascinating diagrams immediately.

Stumbling upon that book was a moment of profound creative insight. And though my rational mind still is unable to grasp the full significance of the golden rectangle, I have used it in every project since, each time with remarkable results. The spaces feel different, hitched in some way to the primordial mystery of creation and a geometric expression of growth and beauty.

For Prana del Mar, we used the golden rectangle everywhere, scaling it up to inform the layout of entire buildings and scaling it down to inform the design of individual elements such as stepping stones, curve changes on the balcony railings, window placements, even the height and diameter of the circular planters, the parts harmonizing with the whole like an elegant conch shell. Using a particularly intriguing diagram from *The Power of Limits* that illuminated the complex organizing principles underlying seemingly random designs, I laid out the elements of the pool deck by superimposing the rock placements and rake lines of one of Japan's most famous Zen gardens, the Ryoanji garden near Kyoto, Japan.

When Erik first approached me about the new building, he said that he was considering putting in a yurt down by the western sand dune. That idea was quickly nixed. Having built several yurts already, and having stayed in them for weeks on end, I knew how susceptible they were to heat fluctuations, especially without shade. Shortly thereafter, he came up with a basic program for the new building: 65-74 square meter (700-800 square foot) practice room, two treatment rooms, one bathroom, an entrance patio, and a mechanical room. The only location that remained within close proximity to the rest of the facilities was a small patch of land adjacent to the main parking lot. In that compact space, bordered by the arroyo to the north, a *ciruelo* tree and the roadway to the west, another *ciruelo* to the east, and the dust and noise of the main parking lot to the south, we began contemplating the building's layout.

Once the program and the location were established, Erik gave me the go ahead. In early May, I began making sketches, using the golden rectangle, the existing treatment rooms, the existing vegetation, and the sun's daily journey to drive the design. Erik's request for a 25 x 40–foot room matched almost exactly the dimension of the golden rectangle and mirrored the southern flank of the Community Building. The distance of the new building from the Community Building was also an exact match. Filled with enthusiasm by these initial findings, I made quick drawings, exploring various ways of using space in relation to the light at various times of day, private functions (such as the treatment rooms and bathroom) versus more public functions (the main practice space), and how to draw people into the building and guide them through the space. I also explored ways of getting light into the building with views in certain directions, while closing off the building to the noise and traffic of the parking lot.

At some point while playing with various schematics, the driving concept for the new building appeared in a flash, a perfect counterpoint to all that we'd done thus far. Instead of expanding outward what about a building that would be unmistakably introverted? What about designing a building that turned inward on itself, offering no views of the surrounding landscape, but still allowing the daily journey of the powerful Mexican sunlight to play itself out in the interior? What about a building that gave the visitors and teacher a place to go inward, where they were guided into an experience of noticing the light itself, and not just the objects lit by the light?

Soon after that moment of clarity the name appeared: The Light Box. On May 11, 2011, I sent Erik five schematics and wrote:

Since all your other buildings are externally oriented and this one's main views are to a parking lot and to a parcel of land whose future is uncertain, I created spaces that exploit a sense of not knowing where you are—no references to the landscape—while playing with that awesome Mexican natural light. All the schematics are made in some way to amaze, washing walls with light, creating links between the ground and the sky, perhaps even creating, on that special day, at that special time, a profound moment of transcendence.

By the time I was done with the five schematics, the idea of the Light Box was resounding in my mind as something ineffable and clear at the same time, something that had undeniably altered my perspective toward a heretofore unforeseen opportunity.

In retrospect, the insight to design a light box wasn't single or isolated, but the product of other insights I'd had in the past, including my discovery of *The Power of Limits* and my fascination with the golden rectangle, my experiences of touring the works of Luis Barragán and his indescribable use of light and color, the structures I'd already designed on the land, and my own love of the particular strength and brilliance of desert sunlight. Like a single wave shaped by the winds, the tides, the curious properties of water, and the shoreline itself, the insight wasn't a single thing but a result of innumerable factors, another ode to interdependence.

Still, with all these things in place, it was now up to Erik, Antonio, and myself to take the insightful experience and turn it into a functioning structure, one that would fit in with the other buildings, delight the guests, and fulfill the requirements of visiting teachers, one that could be easily maintained and comfortably conditioned, and one that could withstand the shaking of earthquakes and the gale force of hurricanes. In other words, it was up to the three of us to shape the building to reflect the best of what art, science, and religion had to offer.

Erik took a week to digest all that I'd sent him, then, as he'd done throughout the previous phases of the project, sent me a long, thorough email clearly expressing his likes, dislikes, and concerns. As a designer, I never believe that my ideas are the final word in anything. With Erik's dedication to the success of the project, he consistently brought new clarity, exposing my oversights and revealing new opportunities. From his comments, the building began to take on its basic orientation:

* The practice room would go on the west side, closest to the Community Building and the treatment rooms on the east.

* The practice room itself would have a shrine at the west end lit by an unseen skylight.

* The ceiling lights would form an inverted Zen garden, with Chinese lanterns of various sizes, thereby drawing a link between the new practice room and the layout of the existing pool deck.

* A band of ground level windows looking out at a secret garden on the south side was to be paired with a band of matching skylights above the north wall to wash it with light.

* A single, square skylight would be set at a diagonal and centered over the vanishing point of the golden rectangle, a vanishing point known in the Middle Ages as "The Eye of God."

* And out of all these decisions, a new driving concept emerged for the practice room itself, a theme that we've explored throughout this book: Heaven and Earth.

I reworked the drawings to reflect these new "certainties." And in the space between "certainties" new questions and differences of opinions arose. I pushed for high ceilings in the practice room, arguing that we needed them to be around 15 feet for the natural light to have room to bounce around, for the proportions to feel right, and for the Chinese globes on the ceiling above not to feel imposing. Erik presented a different and equally valid argument, saying that if the ceilings were too high, the space wouldn't feel intimate and would consume too much energy to heat in the morning, which was a huge factor considering the entire project was off the grid. I countered, saying that the space was crying for radiant in-floor heat, a high-efficiency heating system using hot water in pipes to turn the whole concrete floor into a heater. But Erik's sister, the same one who'd set the environment for Erik's initial insight, had planted a different seed in Erik's mind regarding radiant in-floor heat: A pipe in a radiant heat system she'd installed in her home cracked, spilling water into the home's interior and causing costly damage.

Erik had other concerns. Would the low windows take up too much valuable wall space for teachers wanting to use it for their workshops? Would the long skylight along the north wall produce too much light and heat during the day? How would they stand up during a hurricane? The hidden garden, which I'd enclosed using the same sweeping curves as the western edge of the pool deck, seemed too wide in some places and too squat in others. The unadorned curving wall fronting a windowless building also left Erik uneasy. I envisioned it as a blank canvas for the light and shadows of the adjacent plants to play themselves out upon. Erik felt it would look too spare and become the unsightly black sheep of the center. And though the treatment rooms matched the exact proportions of the golden rectangle, they were tighter than what Erik wanted. Furthermore, with nothing but skylights in those treatment rooms, how would therapists control the light and air flow for their clients?

All these features cost money, and money was a central issue. At the end of Erik's long list of concerns he wrote, "You may have to rename this design Heaven and Hell. I think we're getting closer, but we have to be very careful about adding greater expense. I know I have to reinvest for it to pay off down the line, but I still need this place to start generating some real income so it can pay down my debt and start making more financial sense."

Based on Erik's concerns, I got back to work, doing my best to balance wonder and amazement with practicality, water tightness, and financial efficiency. Leaning again on the mysterious power of the golden rectangle, I divided both the band of skylights above the north wall and the windows to the secret garden into four smaller sections with solid, golden squares in between, thus lowering both the cost and the windows' susceptibility to hurricane damage. I made the lower windows into golden rectangles and centered them at the eye level of a person seated in meditation. Using a lovely trick I'd seen in Luis Barragán's home, I bumped out the frames around those low windows to make the walls appear much thicker, which had the added bonus of preventing sunlight from beaming down directly on the bamboo floor.

For the sake of practicality, I chose to break out of the confines of the golden rectangle and my original vision of a windowless box with a single entrance. I increased the size of the treatment rooms to match those in the Community Building and added windows that could be more readily accessed than the skylights. Because these windows faced away from the most public parts of the retreat center, and since the *ciruelo* tree was located on that side, the visual intrigue of a windowless building was, from most angles, maintained. And instead of the single, monolithic box I'd previously envisioned to cut costs, I lowered the floor of the practice studio from the main hallway to follow the slope of the land, raised the secret garden to the level of the low windows, and divided the roof line into two main sections, the high section over the studio and the low section over the hallway, the bathroom, and the smaller, more intimate treatment rooms. Near the front door, I added peep holes to the secret garden using a scaled down version of the vertical window pattern I'd used on the Community Building's circulation tower. Using the same wide arcs from the pool deck, I reworked the planters and seating near the entrance in order to draw curious guests toward the single wooden door, a feature that I gleefully proclaimed to Erik as "The Roach Motel of Enlightenment." And to fully welcome the guests inside, I borrowed space from the two northwest corners of the treatment rooms to make triangular entrance nooks to those rooms, and, most importantly, to conceal the entrance to the bathroom. Instead of a toilet being the first thing people saw when they entered the building, guests would see a sunlit statue centered at the end of the hall— Hindu elephant god, Ganesha, remover of obstacles.

By mid-July, we had the bulk of the floor plans, elevations, and sections designed. By the end of July, I'd diagramed and arranged the Chinese lanterns and the electrical supply boxes, drawn out the rest of the electrical plan and diagramed the plumbing. I completed the roof drawings to reflect both the layout of the solar panels and the drainage pathways for the seasonal rains. The debate around the ceiling height continued until we finally settled on 12 feet. I completed the drawings in early August and sent them off for final review. Celebrating both the project's outcome and the fact that I'd gotten it in on time, I headed off for my annual backpacking retreat in the High Sierras.

The Language of Creativity
Across Science, Art, and Religion

In the course of this book, I have divided the Path of Creativity into three subgroups: insight, manifestation, and Self-expression. In order to appreciate the universal nature of creativity in all of human endeavors, it is useful to take a few moments to clarify how my definitions of creativity intersect the particular languages used in the domains of science, art, and religion.

In the domain of science, insight is known as **divergent thinking,** that way of knowing that seems to jump the tracks of normal thought. Manifestation involves **convergent thinking,** our capacity to stay focused on discrete tasks in order to bring a project into being. The union of divergent and convergent thinking is known as **paradox,** something that seems self-contradictory or absurd but in reality expresses a possible truth. Think of the colors of a rainbow, for example. When they are expressed on a color wheel, the colors fold back around on themselves, running around in an infinite circle. But when we look at the electromagnetic spectrum, we see color has a linear progression, each gradation of color expressing a different frequency, from red at the low end to violet at the top. Thus, color has a paradoxical nature: It can be seen as *both* a continuous wheel that folds perfectly back on itself *and* a linear progression with two borders—infrared and ultraviolet—at either end.

In the domain of religion, the experience of insight is known as **wisdom**. Like a glass full of muddy water that is set on a counter, wisdom comes from allowing things to settle out so that one can experience the clarity of the liquid that is always there. Manifestation is the practice of **compassion**, the act of working for the benefit of others. And the union of wisdom and compassion is sometimes known as **nonduality**, a word meaning "not two," a reference to the fundamental "oneness" of everything. Like the paradox in science, nonduality rests in the tension of the passive and the active, the feminine and the masculine, the transcendent and the imminent, and is beyond the constraints of good and bad. Curiously enough, some of the most advanced religious practices, such as the Tibetan Buddhist practices of Dzogchen and Mahamudra, are also the most simplistic; they've been designed to get the practitioner to reclaim their natural creativity by being free of constraint or elaboration. One doesn't meditate, or analyze, or conceptualize; one simply is.

Mediating between the domains of science and religion, we discover art and artistic expression. Insight in art is known as **inspiration**. Like an inhalation, inspiration has a quality of something coming to the artist from outside. The active part of art I call **craft**, the accumulated experience, effort, and refinement of working with the materials, equipment, or techniques that allow the artist more choice and range in how he or she expresses those ineffable inspirations. The early works of Picasso, for example, both developed and proved his craft, paving the way for the significance of his latter works. By proving to the world early on that he could produce realistic renderings of human forms, cityscapes, and the natural world, his experiments with cubism weren't viewed as some strange oddity but as a serious attempt to explain an alternative, aperspectival reality. In the pregnant space between inspiration and craft we find **artistic expression,** which is the essence of Self-expression working in the domain of art.

INDIVIDUAL	INSIGHT	SELF-EXPRESSION	MANIFESTATION	COLLECTIVE
SPIRIT	WISDOM	NONDUALITY	COMPASSION	RELIGION
MIND	INSPIRATION	ARTISTIC EXPRESSION	CRAFT	ART
BODY	DIVERGENT THINKING	PARADOX	CONVERGENT THINKING	SCIENCE

All of these aspects return us, yet again, to the three defining aspects of the Ground of Creativity. Luminous dynamism, especially the truth of impermanence, relates to the cycle of life as experienced by our corporal bodies and the ever-evolving, ever-changing truths held by science. Miraculous interplay reminds us that in order to live a truly creative, truly artistic life that we must avoid self-absorption. Miraculous interplay also reminds us to keep connecting with the world around us and not to become transfixed by our thoughts, which leads to isolation. And mysterious complexity relates to spirit and the innovations of religion, our ineffable connection to unknowable Self and the primordial ground of creative insight.

My hope in outlining the specific language of creativity is to show that creativity is not relegated to just a few, rarified aspects of human endeavors. It pervades everything we do. Furthermore, to live a truly creative life means drawing upon the best of what science, art, and religion have to offer while avoiding, to the best of our abilities, the anti-creative activities, such as the tendency to fixate on dogmatic beliefs, also apparent in each of those realms.

A Difference of Opinion

As we have seen, the five qualities of insight and the five qualities of manifestation all appeared at various times over the course of creating the Light Box. What happened next, though, would test the most coveted qualities of Self-expression, the qualities of imagination, wonder, patience, flow, and most especially, love.

While I was away in the mountains, Erik rehired Antonio to work on the Light Box. A robust, friendly, and thoughtful man, Antonio was also trained as a structural engineer. With the freshly completed drawings on the table, Erik and Antonio had their first planning meeting. Antonio began voicing concerns over aspects of the design, concerns that were already in Erik's mind. He proposed cost-cutting measures and new design elements, including making the whole building level instead of stepping down with the topography, further lowering the practice room ceiling to save on additional materials, adding wood elements to the exterior walls, and removing the dramatic sunlit art nook at the end of the hall so as not to borrow space from the treatment rooms.

Upon returning from the mountains, I received an email from Erik noting the pending changes. I was livid.

"He's an engineer" Erik wrote, "so he's echoing some of my feelings about the hallway niche and angled doors. They will probably stay, but I wanted to warn you that you now have two people who aren't completely sold on it." I wasn't convinced and began envisioning all the subtle work of drawing people into the mysterious space only to be met by a toilet bowl. Worse, Antonio suggested putting in a barrel vault, an element that would be more expensive than the roof I'd already designed and had not been used anywhere else in the property.

After raging for a while on my own, I took a breath, and sat down to reply diplomatically. But as I went down the list I just felt myself getting more and more triggered. My Self-expression turned to self-righteousness and I let my words fly.

As the one who you've hired as your architect, whose role is to keep function, aesthetics, and costs in mind, including what you've already built on the property, I've been doing my best to create a space that is inspiring in and of itself and fits into the fabric of your project as a whole.

When I hear someone pitch you an idea like a barrel vault, in a project that has nothing like that anywhere, I feel bad because 1) we start to head in the direction of strange anomalous details that are divorced from the rest of the project and 2) I worry that I'm wasting your money explaining this to you. I really want this to be done in the time I said it would, because I know that finances are tight for you, and I feel worse because I don't feel you trust my judgment as the architect.

Now, after four months, we still haven't solved the main functional issue, which is a warm place to do yoga, and now there is some new, unrelated issue on the table based on the opinion of someone new to the project. This is makes me feel frustrated with myself because I feel like I'm failing at the job you hired me to do.

Exasperated, I added:

All this being said, this is your project, your space, and you have the ultimate say in what you want to do. As your friend and your architect, however, I needed to express this.

To save cost, my suggestion is this: I will make sure all the drawings have Spanish labels, and send them to you in Spanish, and then you can have one of Antonio's draftsmen make the desired changes. I will try to have them by tonight or tomorrow. This will save you money in the long run. It will also leave us a little time for me to do any detail drawing that you may need.

Erik replied shortly thereafter, addressing the ceiling height, the difficulty of getting anyone in the area to give him decent advice on a heating system, and my point of contention on the art nook at the end of the hall.

As you know, that nook forces us to shift the door, which forces us to angle the rear massage room door, which forces us to angle the front massage room door. In order to get one artistic element, we make three other elements—the three entrances—awkward and two of them wasteful of space. Antonio's really not at fault here; he was just articulating all the things that I had been thinking – as well as what a second contractor asked about – when you made that change. I understand your artistic intent, but the functional ramifications aren't insignificant to me. I was trusting you on that because you were insistent, but all the while I still have had nagging doubt. I mean, I don't like staring at the bathroom door any more than you do, but I'm just not sure that it's worth the shake-up and awkwardness to eliminate it.

When I described why you had done it and what you were trying to create—a focal point that draws the viewer in and wasn't a bathroom door—Antonio suggested the small, vaulted ceiling in the hallway. Yes, I know that we don't have this feature anywhere else on the property, but this building is full of things we don't have elsewhere: blank exterior walls, hidden gardens, ground-level windows, steps leading down into a room, Chinese lanterns, etc. He was just making a suggestion as to how we could avoid having to make multiple changes that compromise the function to fit in one art niche.

I also think that you do Antonio a disservice if you think he comes at this just from the perspective of an engineer. He actually has good ideas that have added to the aesthetics of this project on numerous occasions. While he may not be an artist (and neither am I), I often feel that his aesthetic perspective is a sound one. In the end, he was just putting voice to concerns that I already had.

At the end of his cordial email, Erik skillfully held up a mirror to my own frustrations, and though I hadn't totally expected it he agreed to my suggestion: he asked for the drawings. In a flash, I realized that my work on the building was essentially over and that some of what I viewed as the building's strong points might not be realized, instead being either value-engineered or taken in a different direction entirely.

I went to bed angry, got up the next day, gathered all that I'd designed, and sent it off to Mexico. Antonio and his crew built it quickly over the fall, and in early 2012 the first visiting group had the opportunity to utilize the new space.

I Could Never Write a Song But I Can Make a Great Mixed Tape

Artist Ran Ortner, quoting the Catholic mystic Thomas Merton, recently said, "There is nothing as old and tiresome as human novelty; there's nothing as immediate and as new as that which is most ancient, which is always in the process of becoming."

When I look at the images of The Light Box (as I still have yet to visit it in person), I am very proud of what we accomplished. While I was deeply involved in designing the building and while it is something I can rightfully put in my design portfolio, it is misleading to say that the project was somehow solely my own, or even Erik's, Antonio's and mine. The real magic of the project, as is felt in all things that abide for a spell in the manifest realm, is the unending chain of causes and conditions that enabled the building to be brought into existence and that one day will remove it from existence too.

All of which puts a curious twist on the relationship of insight and manifestation. From a conventional view, the experience of insight is a brief moment in time, yet one that provides us with a glimpse of something enduring, something eternal, the felt sense of relatedness and wholeness underlying the illusion of discrete thoughts, ideas, actions, and events. The experience of insight is like throwing open a window on the rolling tides of eternity. Upon the canvas of wholeness, manifestation, which appears to be the most enduring part of the process of creativity, is but a pin prick in the infinite unfolding of time. In our known universe, one that is reputed to be some 13 to 14 billion years old, the whole of human history and its proliferation of products, the stone hand axe, the Pyramids of Egypt, the printing press, the internal combustion engine, the internet, has endured for less than a millionth of a percent of the total history of known time.

A few days after sending off the drawings, I wrote Erik again, this time a letter of apology for my forthrightness.

I awoke feeling sad the last two mornings about my last emails to you.

Being the center and the glue of Prana del Mar, I know that you have a lot on your plate at all times, running the gamut from leaky roofs to squirrely clients. And I know that you are doing all that you can to make the place both financially successful and a memorable experience for all who come to visit.

I am sorry for pushing what I thought was best instead of better listening to your concerns.

If you do want to discuss anything, or would like me to do further work on your project, I would be happy to. And if you have all that you need or find someone to do things for less cost, I am supportive of that, too.

Erik replied, "Thanks, bud, I appreciate it. I completely understand; after all, we're hacking your baby to bits, so I imagine that's frustrating." And though he said he was "hacking my baby to bits," Erik, as the owner of a gorgeous but financially struggling center, was doing his best to make good, long-term decisions, which, in the end, included a lovely mix of my suggestions, Antonio's ideas, and, of course, his own. After all, he'd been developing and living on the grounds for five years. Erik knew the project more intimately than anyone.

While the three principle domains of art, science, and religion describe the various means for approaching a creative challenge, the true test of a project's success is its ability to lead us back to the enduring timelessness of the Ground of Creativity, to some felt sense of dynamism, interdependence, and mysteriousness. The Light Box, I'm pleased to say, shines brightly in all of these areas.[5]

As far as dynamism, the juxtaposition of the overwhelmingly opaque structure among the more open buildings sets up a tension of intrigue. The curving lines leading to the single door draw people into the space. Once inside, Antonio's vaulted ceiling mirrored with

---

[5] Go to www.austinhillshaw.com/projects to see photos and images of the project.

inset river stones on the floor, creates another example of heaven and earth, which, in the face of my vehement protests, I must admit, is stunning. The focal object at the end of the hall is a lovely hand-crafted sink, with the iconography of awakening, the Buddha's head over that sink, mirroring people's basic state of wakefulness. Three small, individually lit, vertical art niches, symbolizing body, mind, and spirit, sit in the space to the side of the bathroom door, providing visual cues for retreat participants to tune into all aspects of their being.

Dropping down into the studio (a feature they kept!) beneath a prominent skylight allows the visitors to sense the slope of the natural topography and enter the practice studio through a pool of light matched on the opposite side by natural light from the hidden skylight pouring over the shrine. The pairing of the four operable skylights with the four low-lying windows again illuminates the natural balance of heaven and earth, while, on a practical level, allows for stacked ventilation: The hot air leaving through the skylights allows fresh air to be pulled in from the low-lying windows. The odd lowness of the windows sets up another tension, which is resolved only when a visitor finds himself seated, perhaps in a contemplative mood, when an unexpected garden comes into view.

So, too, with interdependence. Erik didn't have to invent the idea of a retreat center, Antonio didn't have to create masonry block, concrete, and rebar, and I didn't have to come up with skylights, entry sequences, or the golden rectangle. Nor did we have to invent the overwhelming majority of tools we used to communicate our ideas and concerns to one another. Nor did we have to create the strong, skilled hands of all the workers and subcontractors, all of them arriving on the project with their own unique constellations of families and responsibilities, gifts and challenges, all leaving their own indelible marks on the project. Even the idea of a light box, though it appeared as something fresh and novel at the time, reflected the driving concept of a project I'd worked on a decade earlier for a Boulder, Colorado-based photographer. That project was designed by a friend of mine from my undergraduate days at Berkeley, Mike Moore, the same person who inspired me to attend architecture school in the first place, cofounder and principle of the cutting-edge design build firm Tres Birds Workshops in Denver.

In an intimately interdependent universe, the material objects and conceptual frameworks were already in place, waiting for our unique lenses on the world, and all the friction, heat, and sparks that arise when those lenses rub up against one another, waiting for us to leave our singular fingerprints on the reconfiguring of wholeness. And, in our little building arising near the tip of Baja, California, we had the rare and precious opportunity to participate in the formation of something derived from all these givens, something that would emerge totally unique.

And finally, mystery is in the project, especially the mystery of light and shadow, the mystery of a proportioning system that, like DNA itself, contains codes for growth, beauty and a sense of vitality, and the mystery of conscious self-awareness, that strange and wonderful capacity that allows us to walk the Path of Creativity. The inviting patio to a single door of an apparently windowless building sets up a sense of intrigue. The low windows on the south side of the building and the matching skylights on the north underscore the ever-present influences of Earth and Heaven, a path that has evolved from the tension between the two, between the magic and intrigue of thoughts, emotions, and dreams and the solidity and responsiveness of animate matter, between the omnipotence of disembodied beings and the instincts of animals, between the spark of insight that makes room for something new and the confidence of our established skills and abilities.

The seemingly thick walls and the absence of views allow guests to feel safe and invites them to come back into their own internal experience, while the Eye of God skylight located at the vanishing point of the golden rectangle highlights the proportioning system itself, revealing the hidden? organizing principle behind the entire project, a proportioning system based on the intrigue of an irrational number, whose decimal places never repeat themselves. And, since the project is a few of kilometers south of the Tropic of Cancer—the line demarking the northern most boundary of the sun appearing directly overhead—for a few months around the summer solstice, at noon, a beam of light shoots down through that skylight, bringing the ineffable qualities of heavenly light into the material realm.

There were other factors at play that led to the success of the project. The first was a quality of what Zen Master Suzuki Roshi deemed "beginner's mind." For Erik, Antonio Manriquez, and I, Prana del Mar was the largest project any of us had tackled. . Though we all had some experience and expertise in our fields, none of us pretended to be an expert. As a result, we all felt comfortable sharing our opinions and listening to each other, arguing our points, then letting them go when it became clear that someone else's idea was better. We all learned a great deal through such a process and improved our skills as we went along. We all contributed to the success of the project and we all made mistakes. And despite what our initial roles in the project might have suggested, we were all involved in the creative process.

Erik told me recently; "I could never write a song, but I can make a great mixed tape." The reality is that everyone, even the most celebrated creative's throughout history, are making mixed tapes too. We all draw upon the creations of people who've come before us.

Next was humor. Amid the necessarily thorough but sometimes tedious email exchanges, Erik and I got into the habit of setting trip wires of humor. On more than one occasion, using the cover of clean drawings and mechanical lettering, I would diagram schematics of members of Erik's family in cages next to some architectural element. Based on our two conflicting color preferences, myself enjoying the bright colors of Luis Barragán and his inclination towards the more contemplative Spanish Missionary Style, we'd purposely search for images berating the value of the other person's tastes, sending the worst of those particular styles we could find to one another.

Finally, and most importantly, there was love—not like, not pleasantness, but love. Inevitably, with a project of this size and scale, with thousands of minor and major decisions, we agreed on a lot of things. But we also had our differences, all of which were valid, and often impassioned opinions. And even though we became angry and frustrated with one another, even when we didn't get our way, we respected one another and recognized the value that each of us brought to the project. If Erik and I weren't defaming one another's family members in the closing lines, we almost always closed our emails with that simple, powerful, four-letter word: love.

Reinterpreting Huston's description of the historic Jesus Christ, on any collaborative project it is more important to love than to be right.

The external purpose of creativity may be to envision a project and bring it into some sort of fruition. And, as we have already begun to touch upon, the inward journey can be arduous and messy. When surrendered to, as opposed to thinking that creativity should be some sort of pleasure cruise on the Queen Mary, it can be unfathomably rewarding. Any genuinely creative undertaking, especially those that unfold over long periods of time, is always paired with the internal opportunity to untie our own knots, the knots of imprints, the knots of habitual patterns, a chance to confront self-defeating obstacles so that life-enabling Self-expression can flow more freely.

In this next chapter, the concluding chapter, we'll address this full force.

PULLING IT ALL APART:
MOONLIGHT ON THE MOUNTAINS

It's true the wind blows terribly here
but moonlight also leaks between
the roof planks of this ruined house.
—Izumi Shikibu

Halfway up the Berkeley Hills, along the route of a historic and long-defunct streetcar line and an even more historic and intermittently active geological fault, at the confluence of three creeks that join together beneath Codornices Park and emerge united at the focal point of the Berkeley Rose Gardens, in a grove of stately redwoods surrounding a turn-of-the-century house, in one of its seven apartments, in a ship's prow of a bedroom, half of which rested on the apartment below, half of which was cantilevered out into space, upon a double mattress set upon the hardwood floors, in a tangle of a sheets and bedding, my girlfriend and I, unbeknownst to us, conceived a child. It was right around the spring equinox. We'd only moved into the apartment two weeks earlier. In such an idyllic setting, in a world-renowned city facing the Golden Gate, in a historic home abutting one of the most beautiful parks I'd ever seen, it might have seemed perfect.

From the street, our building looked like a typical, single-family home. Built during the East Bay exodus, when thousands fled the devastation of the Great San Francisco Earthquake and Fire of 1906, it was symmetrical, complete with two large-pane glass windows and wide steps leading up to a generous porch covered by a prominent gable. As you moved around to the sides, however, the ground began to drop away, revealing a second story underneath, and then a third below that. Moreover, the conversion of the building into five one-bedroom apartments and two studios, including a lower basement apartment accreted on to the southeast corner, caused the growth of tumor-like enclosures for additional hot-water heaters, electrical meters, gas lines, laundry facilities, and all of the additional plumbing, much of which ran outside the exterior walls. When you stood in the back parking lot, the building loomed overhead, an architectural Rubik's Cube with no help of reordering, the only unifying factor being a fresh coat of light grey paint. Even the foundation was dubious. The contractor living next door claimed that our houses were built on a "mud glacier," a term I'd never encountered in all my years of studying the geomorphology, but which, along with the Hayward Fault nearby, fittingly described the causes behind the equally prominent crack dividing the front steps into two distinct halves and doors that would suddenly refuse to open.

It was April Fools' Day, 2009, when we found out Jen was pregnant, a day that was already significant for both of us. For Jen, it was the 21-year anniversary of her first period, which she remembered quite vividly; she thought her younger brother was playing an April Fools' joke on her, staining the toilet with ketchup, perhaps, to make it look like blood. For me, it marked the 13-year anniversary of the death of my best friend from college, Matt Baxter, whom I'd met at the University just down the street. Although he was just a novice himself, he taught me how to rock climb, and we forged our friendship climbing throughout the Bay Area and our beloved Yosemite, where he died in 1996 during a solo ascent on El Capitan. I had spent the earlier part of the evening outside with some men friends of mine, gathered around a fire, recounting the memory and significance of the loss of my dear friend. When I came home and sat down at the Craigslist dining room table we'd bought a week earlier, Jen placed two pregnancy test sticks in front of me. Both were marked positive. She might as well have walloped me with a sledge hammer.

The news might have come across better if not for one crucial detail: Jen and I fought frequently, with great intensity, and for hours, sometimes days at a time. Our fighting wasn't a small part of our relationship, an occasional moment of tension over some miscommunication, a brief but reasonable flaring of tempers normal among couples. No, in my mind our fighting was a different beast all together, two beasts really, two beasts immune to any possible reconciliatory etiquette, tearing one another apart in long drawn-out campaigns. We each made vicious attacks and counter-attacks on each other's character, the other's families' characters, and the others friends' characters. Our fights were full of cursing and screaming, objects hurled at one another, crippling battles with shaky and fleeting moments of reconciliation, only to be followed by another underhanded comment, or passive-aggressive stab, and we'd be at war once again. And though I was blind to it at the time, my whole campaign to keep her at a distance was waged with the unspoken goal of avoiding what I really feared most: the possibility of true intimacy.

Sitting around our new used dining table that evening, we were both in a state of shock. The idea of bringing an innocent child into such an environment left us both profoundly uneasy. That night, we stayed up into the wee hours, debating and blaming, drowning each other with new oceans of fear.

In the seven months we'd been together, I believed our relationship to be as dysfunctional as they come, the sort of thing that would leave a daytime television producer salivating. Yet even under such circumstances, with ample opportunities for either one of us to walk away, we'd stuck it out, sensing that there was something important to be discovered. And the child, at least the idea of the child, like a light in the distance, somehow made sense to me. As Jen, an impeccable planner with a lightning-quick mind, machine-gunned off possible scenarios, and as I struggled to keep up, my own fears and disbelief hurling themselves against the shorelines in my head, my mind would quiet for a moment as I thought of the baby, those cells that were dividing in the womb of this woman in front of me, the wide-eyed woman waving her arms and screaming. After more than 12 hours of violent emotional outbursts and fragmented planning, Jen said, "You're the man, you decide."

OPPOSITES IN OPPOSITION

Jen and I could not have been more opposite. She had a warm, engaging personality and loved spending time with people. I was more reserved, comfortable on the peripheries of the action, even being described by my dear friend from birth as aloof. Jen was half-Filipino, half-Pennsylvania Dutch with a trace of Native American ancestry, which prompted her to say when angered, "You can kiss my half-yellow ass!" I was about as Caucasian American as they come: both my mother's family and my father's had been around since the Revolution and fought on opposite sides of the Civil War. Jen trained in clairvoyance at the Berkeley Psychic Institute and read my thoughts and emotions better than I could. I had gone to UC Berkeley, studied geography and rhetoric, graduated with honors and forged my identity as an arrogant intellectual snob. She was ambitious and had owned and operated two wellness centers by the time she was 27. I lumbered along with mine, doing all that I could to keep expenses down, possessions to a minimum, and have ample time to read, write, surf, climb, and meditate. Her memory was practically photographic, except for the shape-shifting photo paper she developed it on. Mine was more like a sand painting, laboriously coming to some cohesive understanding, then losing it all with the slightest of breezes. She taught workshops on intimacy and couple's massage. I avoided such workshops like the plague, preferring an individualist approach to growth and liberation that confounded even my Buddhist teacher.

Along with the opposition, however, there was also dynamic polarity, the strong pull of those opposed to one another, the swooning qualities of a high-voltage electric field, the warbling of space due to the force of attraction, the voice of a reconciliatory universe saying, "Hey, take a look at this!"

Fulfilling a longstanding fantasy of mine, we'd met in the heavenly chaos of a late night dance pit, at the Bay Area's most recent affront to America's longstanding puritanical shadow, Burning Man, one of the few places left where cell phones don't work, where art—beautiful, inspired, temporary art—is everywhere, and people gather en masse to watch the sunrise. The music that night combined two genres of electronic music: *dubstep*, a raw, stripped-down genre using slow, grinding rhythms and ultra low-frequency bass riffs;

and *glitch*, an eclectic assemblage of sonic clips, shards, and scraps, like pieces of broken ceramic arranged into a beautiful mosaic. The overall affect of the two genres created a delectable sonic cataclysm, the walls of sound crumbling from the speakers, luxurious primordial riffs swaying the willing dancers like harbored ships in a tsunami. Furthering the sense of buoyancy, I had just returned from my annual backpacking trip in the Eastern Sierra three days earlier. My most treasured time of the year, I'd spent six nights alone above timberline, doing what I loved most: reading, writing, meditating, swimming in clear, bone-chilling water, and watching the moon rise over the craggy peaks, spilling its mystical light over the white granite bones of the earth.

Swaying in the waves of sound pouring from the speakers, kicking up clouds of dust at our feet, with her enchanting smile and sparkly, engaging eyes, we were drawn together, so it seemed, by the cosmic winds sweeping the Black Rock desert. We kissed before we knew each other's names and were inseparable thereafter. I named her Chispa Morena, "Dark Spark," and she called me El Matador, "The Killer," and, as newly found soul mates, we began, unknowingly, the arduous task of undoing our longstanding fears and habitual patterns standing in the way of true, rock-meets-bone love.

After our stellar beginning, things went quickly south. In my mind, I tried to reconcile our relationship in a number of ways. Sometimes I thought of our relationship as a trip to the zoo, each of us looking across the bars at one another, wondering who this curious and exotic creature was, the only difference being that there was no barrier, no protection from the gnashing teeth and sharp claws. Sometimes I thought of it like a divine crucible, the heat, pressure, and claustrophobia driving the transformation, the forging of two

very self-centered individuals into more open, tolerant, compassionate members of society. Other times I saw it like those creeks outside our window, the confluence of karmic streams, the swirling and
turbulence ultimately weaving into a unified force. And other times
I saw us like meteors bouncing along in the upper atmosphere, in
real danger of burning up from all the friction with only the most
miniscule of chances that some part of us would touch down safely
on terra firma.

As time wore on, we stockpiled a formidable scrap heap of bad
behavior toward one another and the relationship became more and
more antagonistic. I saw her as an incorrigible, man-hating narcis-
sist with an annoying knack for self promotion, a half-yellow witch
whose ravaged island of origin had contributed one and one word
only to the English language, *amok*—mad with a murderous frenzy.
She saw me as arrogant and passive-aggressive, a socially inept
man-child in his late thirties who'd been traumatized by his parent's
divorce in the first few years of his life, an irredeemable misogynist
at war with the divine feminine.

Both of us had valid points. Jen was often incorrigible. Even
when I tried my best, she would easily find something to blame me
for, consistently pointing out that I hadn't a clue how to treat or,
more precisely, to honor a woman. And I was often unreachable. On
those particularly bad nights, when I felt at the frayed frontiers of
wit's end, instead of trying to patch things up so as not to go to bed
enraged, I would demand that I sleep in the front room, next to the
shrine, on the mattress I kept in my van, in the sleeping bag I took
to the wilderness.

I'd never fought so much in my life as I had during the first seven
months of our relationship. During my time alone, in the wake of

another battle, hiding out in the park or lost in the Berkeley Hills, I often found myself with my head buried in my hands, either numb with a tension headache or sobbing uncontrollably in disbelief.

Yet there we were, the morning after April Fool's Day, both under slept and emotionally exhausted, our DNA irrefutably entwined and growing in her belly.

"You're the man," she said "you decide."

AN IRREFUTABLE MESSAGE

Being the man, I did what seemed most natural to me at the time: I grabbed one of those pregnancy sticks, got in my car, drove over the Bay Bridge, and headed to Grace Cathedral. There, just in front of the building, in a discrete appendage of a courtyard, was my destiny, the interfaith labyrinth, an aesthetically and functionally mind-blowing form, a form which I'd begun to explore in earnest a few months earlier as a method, like meditation, for promoting creative insight subverting the confines of linear thinking.

Labyrinths are ancient archetypes. Their precise origins are unknown. But they can be found in various forms in cultures throughout the world. The 11-circuit labyrinth evolved in Europe during the Middle Ages as a substitute for the dangerous pilgrimage to the Holy Land. The labyrinth gets its name from its layout of 11 concentric circles around a center with six flower-like petals. Differing from a maze, labyrinths contain no dead ends, false starts, or misdirections. The only choice is whether or not to enter. A single prescribed path winds its way through the entirety of the concentric circles, making 28 180° turns on the way to the center, thus aligning one with the 28 days of the lunar cycle. Once in the center, one lingers for a spell, possibly gaining some insight, then follows the same path out to the initial starting place.

When I arrived at the edge of the labyrinth, I formulated my question, which, looking back on it now seems a bit strange. Instead of asking, "Should we have the child?" I asked, "What to do about our relationship?"

With my first step, I felt the world shift. As I wound my way around the concentric circles, the first things to come to mind were those I had loved and lost. I thought of my grandmother, Elizabeth Binyon Smith—Mammaw as she was known to her grandkids— who I'd been very close to and lost in 2004. I thought of Matt Baxter and his death at the age of 26. I thought of my stillborn nephew, Ely Clarkson Shaw—a perfect child with the unmistakable face of my younger brother.

As I continued, winding my way along the outer peripheries of the labyrinth, my mind settled on a more universal mantra, the first of the four famed Buddhist reminders, precious human birth:

Contemplate the preciousness of being born free and well favored. This is difficult to gain and easy to lose. Now I must do something meaningful.

As I snaked along the sensuous curves of the labyrinth, the words fell away. I simply felt at peace.

The final stretch of the labyrinth has one walk along the outer-most circle before walking the final straightaway to the center. It's like a moment of respite in the deep space of the outermost ring, a pregnant pause before completing the final turn and entering the center. Several feet before I actually entered the center, I was struck, so it seemed, by rainbow lightning, and a single word was set in my consciousness: *MARRIAGE.*

For much of my adult life I had cultivated and coveted mystical experience, those moments where the world seems to turn itself inside out, revealing its true essence beyond the buzzing static of discursive thinking. And during my times as a rock climber, a surfer, and a meditator, I'd had many such experiences, the dawning of insight cracking my mind.

But not one of those experiences was anything like this.

As I stood in the center, with my eyes closed and my arms by my side, I felt a current of energy running through my body, as though I were a lightning rod connecting heaven and earth. Sweat poured from my skin and water shot from my eyes. The sweat was neither hot nor cold and the tears were neither sadness nor joy. It was pure experience, sensation and emotion, the creative life-force energy coursing through me. In my mind's eye, that energy moved up and down the conduit of my body, swirling as two rainbow vortexes in the space behind my eyes.

As I stood there longer, I felt exhilaration and terror precipitating out of the pure, life-force energy, dancing with equal abandon with my limitless potential as a human being and my lifelong habits and defense structures. I sat cross-legged and surrendered to the feeling: the absolute, ineffable truth leading me in an irrefutable direction. I sat there in awe, savoring the universe's willingness to deliver a message to me with such clarity.

After some time I stood up and decided to envision the child entering the world. I took a moment to stand in each of the six florets surrounding the center, letting the florets represent the sheaths of existence. Stepping from one to the next, I imagined the child as an absolute presence, then a spirit, then a soul, then a mind, then a personality, and, finally, as a physical being entering this world.

Before walking out, I let out a lion's roar, a primal scream of determination to welcome and protect this child. On the last stretch of the path, a stiff wind threatened to blow me over. But I righted my balance, exited, and looked up, the clear spring sky and the luminous flags snapping in the distance atop the Fairmont and Mark Adam hotels. I went to the gift shop below the cathedral, bought two labyrinth pendants, then drove back to the East Bay and home, where I walked Chispa Morena down to the Rose Garden and asked for her hand in marriage.

She agreed, we embraced, and we entered into a dream-like stretch of love, support, and appreciation for one another, all of which lasted two whole days, two whole days of bliss concluded by my first bona fide panic attack.

THE LONG UNDOING

I heard somewhere that during a pregnancy, expectant parents go through their own personal challenges, the necessary psychological and spiritual adjustments in order to prepare themselves to be a mother or father. While Jen's changes were dominated by the ceaseless bodily transformations and physical discomforts, mine were overwhelmingly psychological, frequented by panic attacks, binge behavior, and manic-depressive episodes. Over time, in place of Chispa Morena and El Matador, Jen became the "The Puker" and I, "The Crier."

If our lives before our pregnancy were difficult, life during the pregnancy felt like a stream of cataclysms, fueled by Jen's hormonal surges and the alien being growing inside her, and my own profound terror of being a husband, a father, and, most paralyzing of all, a provider. I had spent the last two decades doing all that I could to avoid commitment and responsibility. Even architecture projects that fell into my lap made me edgy as I knew that I would be tied to a particular place and a particular client for the duration of the project.

On an outer level, we began making some strides as a team, exploring birthing options and strategizing as we attempted to utilize our resources and every inch of our compact, one – bedroom apartment. The newly purchased dining room table and an ornate credenza were re-recycled on Craigslist. We upgraded to a queen sized mattress and purchased a solid bed frame with storage to go underneath. Jen's parents bought us a rocking chair and placed it in the corner by the balcony window. We hired a midwife, teamed up with a prenatal group, and signed up for Hypnobirthing classes. Jen secured baby clothing and equipment on parent networks and from other young moms she knew. We spent weekends going to furniture showrooms and the behemoth Emeryville IKEA, and I spent hours assembling all the components and securing them to the unlevel floors and catawampus lath-and-plaster walls of our 800-square-foot apartment.

Jen, with her lightning-fast mind and her need for data, bought 15 books on pregnancy and parenting, which she would consult and cross-reference. I bought nothing and barely read the book she pushed on me, defiantly swearing by the famed pediatrician Dr. Spock's opening lines to his book on parenting: "You know more than you think you do," which I'd come across only as an example of engaging first lines in a book on writing.

But the inner preparation was far more messy and arduous. As Jen's belly grew and the apartment transformed, we continued to butt up against self-defeating patterns, deep-seated fears, and unhealed wounds. During our first ultrasound, for example, I sat there frozen in the low-lit treatment room as the nurse rolled the sensor over Jen's belly, taking measurements with a white cursor and typing them into the computer. At the end she presented us with a grainy, black and white photo like a transmission from deep space: strange block-shaped numbers along the sides of a central image of what looked like an egg, sunny side up, caught in a tractor beam. I maintained my glacial composure until we got to the car, where, staring at the photo, I broke into tears wailing, "We are not ready for this!"

Soon after the ultrasound, Jen signed us up for an internet service that sent us weekly updates chronicling the miracle of life. But that's not how they landed for me. Like the central commander of a besieged nation, I read those updates with the horror of watching the perimeter defense structure beginning to crumble. Not unlike the ultrasound, the images, especially the early ones, looked like photos from some underwater probe deep in the Mariana Trench.

The accompanying text was equally unnerving:

Week 5: At this point your baby's about the size of a sesame seed and looks more like a tiny tadpole... his tiny heart begins to divide into chambers and beat and pump blood.

Week 6: Baby about the size of a lentil and the bud of tissue that gives rise to his lungs has appeared.

Week 7: Your baby's about the size of a blueberry. The tail will disappear in a few weeks but that's about the only thing getting smaller.

Each time a new notification appeared in my inbox, I was hesitant to even open it. The whole thing seemed so confounding, surreal, and terrifying.

A month after our first ultrasound, I coaxed Jen into going to a one-night return showing of one of my all time favorite movies, Stanley Kubrick's interpretation of Stephen King's *The Shining*. As we sat there in the dark theater, however, the movie seemed eerily autobiographical: A failed writer of a husband and his lonely, emotionally malnourished wife holed up for the winter in a high mountain resort, only to be undone by cabin fever, the husband's own demons, and the resort's tragic and haunted past. Even the final chase scene, where the psychic boy is being chased by his deranged, hatchet-wielding father through the maze, seemed like a twisted mirror to my luminous experience inside the labyrinth, casting my decision to have the baby beneath a shadow of doubt. "What the hell was I thinking, consulting a Christian archetype," I thought, "I'm a goddamn Buddhist!"

Shortly after seeing *The Shining*, Jen and I sustained another blow. One of her massage and coaching clients and my new writing mentor, Dr. Ronald Takaki, a husband, father of three, grandfather of many others, and prolific writer and pioneer of Ethnic Studies programs at UCLA and UC Berkeley, hung himself after battling depression for years. And he did so during the time he was supposed to be in session with Jen.

Earlier that year, in February, through his appreciation for all that Jen had done for his sense of well-being, Ron began to counsel me on my own writing, encouraging me to transform it from heady abstractions of interest to few to concrete stories that would capture the attention of a larger audience. In early May, I had finally reworked a chapter based on his advice and sent it off to him. In the reading room at the Berkeley Public Library, I received his reply:

Dear Austin:

I quickly read your new draft, and want to say thank you for taking my comments on the first draft to heart. What you wrote this time is definitely on track. Many readers will be able to relate to this writing: It tells a story about a real person, real experiences, and a real opening for your readers and architects.

I think you have found your "voice." Keep on telling stories as you write your book.

So, you are off to an audacious start. Keep up the great work,

Ron

A few hours later, I received another email from Ron:

Dear Austin:

I have been thinking about a title for your book: "The Labyrinth of an Awakened Architect."

Anyway, just a suggestion,

Ron

Greatly encouraged, I shared the good news with Jen, but she quickly cast it in an ominous light. "You have to keep feeding him work," she said, "he really needs something to keep his mind occupied."

But I wasn't a fast writer. With Ron's encouragement I'd made a giant stride forward. But it had taken me three months to transform one chapter. Three weeks later, Ron took his life.

Not only did I feel a sense of responsibility, his suicide seemed to underscore the problems of writers in general. Even though Ron had written several highly acclaimed books, had a loving family and thousands of appreciative students, it wasn't enough to overcome his ultimate desire for death, which, along with Jack Nicholson's aspiring writer/hatchet-wielding character, further cast doubt over my own urge to write. Not only was it dubious that my writing would cover the needs of the coming child, I could feel the real possibility of going into a psychotic breakdown or deep depression.

Jen also felt responsible for Ron's suicide. She had worked with him for years, encouraging him to make changes to both his diet and his thought patterns. In his appreciation, he'd even used her middle name, Epiphany, as a play on a title of one of his chapters. Jen later learned from Ron's wife, Carol, who was also Ron's editor, that when she found her husband, Jen's usual $20 tip was left on the dining room table in view of the Japanese maple he'd used to hang himself.

That fall, one day shy of the autumnal equinox, the University of California held a memorial service for Ron in the International House Auditorium. As a testament to his love for his students, the admiration of his colleges, and his dedication to helping others find their own voice, the room was filled to capacity, with many others pouring out into the adjacent hallway. Jen and I wept for most of the service.

There were other shake-ups. In order to focus on being a mom and help us pay for the baby's expenses, Jen put her wellness center on the market, only to be courted by 1) people with no business experience 2) people with no health and wellness experience 3) the legally insane 4) strange combinations of the three. My stepmother, whom I'd known and loved since I was a child, was diagnosed with breast cancer and underwent a double mastectomy. In the midst of the freefall economy, my stepfather, a remarkably kind, generous, and successful man, lost a substantial portion of his savings in a Ponzi scheme, a scheme run by an old friend from high school. Nationwide, the newly elected Obama and his "audacity of hope" were quickly being undone by the quagmire of two wars and the debtor nation unveiling itself at home. At all financial levels and across all walks of life, the American Dream was being undermined by the nightmare of rampant, dangerous greed.

All the while, the strange, destabilizing transmissions just kept on coming:

> **Week 13**: *Your baby's the size of a medium shrimp. If you're having a girl, she now has more than two million eggs in her ovaries.*

> **Week 17**: *Your baby's about the size of an avocado and his eyes have moved closer to the front of his head.*

While Jen gave up all intoxicants to protect the health of the baby, I did just the opposite, increasing my alcohol consumption to try and keep my emotions at bay. On more than one occasion I drank myself to the point of sickness, including one particularly embarrassing outing during my younger brother's bachelor party. On that day, fresh in from sea level, sweltering beneath the fierce high-altitude sun in the outskirts of Denver, totally out of control on prodigious amounts of tequila and Budweiser, I charged over $2000 of strange multimedia art pieces at a music festival, including a skull and a life-sized anatomical skeleton painted garish colors. The next day, with my ongoing worries about money, I begged the artists to retract my order. They insisted I purchase *something*, claiming they would have sold those pieces to someone else had I not reserved them.

I stopped drinking after that, only to take up smoking with Jen's father whenever our families got together.

In September, three months before our due date, Jen ended up in the hospital with early contractions. Undoubtedly, the instability of our relationship coupled with the difficult challenge of running and selling her business had caused her great strain. After that, we did what we could to slow her down, limiting physical activity, including sex, doing all that we could to prevent the child from being born premature. But the sense that we might go into labor at any time added to the general feeling of anxiety.

There was also, of course, the marriage piece. In the beginning, we thought we had enough to think about and therefore would wait until after the child was born. But a close friend of mine, Eliza Kerr, who'd been engaged to Matt Baxter when he died in his climbing accident, said, "If I were you, I'd do it now. It creates stability."

That was in May, and though it seemed like a good idea at the time, driven by my own fear of commitment, it soon became another point of contention in the ongoing debates . After several months, we finally scheduled a date at San Francisco's City Hall, for October 13, 2009, the day after Jen turned 33.

The morning of our appointment, we awoke to a freakish, early winter storm, violent erratic wind and surges of driving rain, coating the streets with leaves, branches, and other debris. We sat at our kitchen table that morning doing, as we always had, debating whether or not this was the right thing to do. Ninety minutes before our scheduled time, we mustered our courage, wrapped ourselves in winter clothes, raced to a Tibetan gift shop on Solano, picked up two knot-of-eternity rings, hers with red inlay symbolizing passion, mine with blue inlay symbolizing aggression (indicative of our various styles of avoidance), and drove over the wind-whipped Bay Bridge to San Francisco City Hall. We filled out the paperwork for the license and waited nervously for our appointment below the soaring cupola, as the building staff set up an earthquake preparedness event commemorating the 1989 Loma Prieta earthquake. Finally, as Jen was beginning to buckle beneath the thought of taking my last name on the forms, a large, jovial lesbian judge with a dental tattoo of a peace sign on her canine called our names, went over the forms, walked us up the steps, and married us, our only witnesses being Peanut, the new, gender-neutral name for our unborn child we'd taken from the internet service, and the commemorative bust of slain city counselor and gay rights activist Harvey Milk.

Once married, I thought we would somehow be rewarded for following through with the decision, that despite all the fighting, puking, and crying, and my reptilian desires to run, we had stuck it out and made it to this divinely inspired milestone. I thought things might stabilize, or at least ease up a bit, that The Puker and The Crier would both feel a little more relaxed as their lives unfolded together.

But we didn't. The economy continued to freefall, the days grew progressively colder and darker, and our nervous anticipation heightened. Other mothers, many of them complete strangers, who'd recently gone through labor would approach Jen, her big belly signpost of pregnancy, and offload their tales of horror. The thrust of my manuscript kept changing, causing me to backtrack again and again. We continued our usual styles of combat, she blaming and attacking, me judging and withdrawing. We retired another relationship counselor. Each morning I would seethe in the kitchen, livid over another, overly precise mandate for some odd food combination. Each night, we would put on god-awful New Age music and practice our Hypnobirthing scripts.

And all the while, the transmissions just seemed stranger and stranger:

Week 26: Your baby's the size of an English Hothouse Cucumber. If you're having a boy, his testicles are beginning to descend into his scrotum, a trip that will take about two to three days.

Week 33: Your baby's the size of a pineapple. She's rapidly losing that wrinkled, alien look and her skeleton is hardening.

On the day before Thanksgiving, a few weeks before Peanut's prognosticated due date, I drove to San Francisco to pick up the birth tub from our sleep-deprived midwife, who was now, , by default, also our newly appointed relationship coach. It was a bluebird day, clear and still, one of the last holdout days of the Indian Summer. After picking up the tub, I headed to the Marin side of the Golden Gate and walked out to the center of the bridge and stared long and hard at the water below. I wasn't feeling suicidal, but I knew this was where over 2000 people had chosen to end their lives. The space around me felt thick and immense, the ethereal beauty of San Francisco, the roaring traffic behind me, and the primordial force of the life-giving, life-taking qualities of the water swirling below.

THE PERIMETER BREACHED

As we entered December I noticed a remarkable shift happening. The late autumn sun began to lower itself in the southern sky, its rays dipping below the lowest branches of the surrounding redwoods, flooding our apartment with light, illuminating the co-sleeper next to our bed, washing over the coffee table, the sofa, and the rocking chair we placed in the corner, the brilliant light and the long shadows cohabitating in our dwelling. I set up the birth tub and we watched movies in it, feeling like third-rate celebrities. Jen continued to grow, and, though it didn't feel that way at the time, so did I.

Even the quality of the transmissions were beginning to turn, talking not only of unfettered growth, but transformation:

Week 39: Your baby's waiting to greet the world! He weighs about 7 pounds, a mini watermelon; the outer layers of skin are sloughing off as new skin forms underneath.

When the due date came and then went, we flipped our vows of celibacy on their head and became tantric rabbits, supplementing our evening Hypnobirthing ritual with good old-fashioned sex. Ten days later Jen received a dangerously low amniotic fluid measurement and we were admitted immediately to Alta Bates hospital on a Friday night. Jen set up the music she wanted, I made Japanese flower arrangements out of the bedpans, and the midwife refereed our disputes. The staff induced labor and we waited, and waited, enduring another tempestuous day and a half of anxiety, frustration, and fear.

Early Sunday morning, on the eve of winter solstice, Jen's cervix finally began to open. For an indeterminable amount of time, I watched the crown of Peanut's head appear, then move in and out, like the shore break on the rising of the tide. Like a totem, my wife squatted on the bed, and my eyes moved back and forth between the awesome determination on her face, indescribably beautiful in both its transcendence and its rooted presence, and the head of our child navigating the birth canal, the room pervaded by a singing presence during this most primordial of creative offerings.

Twenty minutes after dawn, after our seven-month calamitous courtship and another nine months of psycho-hormonal hell for both of us, with the birth canal successfully navigated and the perimeter of my defenses fully breached, our baby, a luminous little girl, was born. We named her Sierra Lucia, a name meaning "moonlight on the mountains."

EMERGENCE

It's ten o'clock on a Thursday evening. The garish art piece I settled upon after my drunken art-buying rampage hangs in the corner. It features a human skeleton about a third its normal size in lotus position, mounted on plywood painted purple and teal, with positive slogans such as "joy," "growth," and "strive" written on its bones. Below the skeleton's feet, written in silver pen, it used to say, "Life is Pure," which I hated. While I was away in the mountains last summer, Jen changed it to "Life is Raw." We've further undermined its sterile purity by pasting Sierra's pen drawings and random photos over the annoyingly positive aphorisms.

Through the door to the balcony, the sky glows like a lantern, a thin marine layer in from the Pacific, lit from above and below. Though I can't see it, I know the moon is nearing full. Sierra doesn't want to go to bed right now and I don't blame her; she just woke up from a late afternoon nap. With the rest of her teeth coming in, seemingly all at once, and an irritation in one of her ears, she hasn't felt well the past couple of days.

"Do you want to go see the moon?" I ask.

"*Moown!*" She squeals, pointing upwards and spinning in my arms to look for it through the glass.

"Yeah? Let's go out and see the moon!"

Jen and I work together, layering warm clothes over our daughter's pajamas, slipping on a pair of boots, sliding her arms into a warm jacket, placing the white knit cap atop her head. She looks adorable, all bundled up with her little legs still wrapped in her pajama bottoms.

As soon as we're out from under the gable, Sierra turns her gaze skyward, looking around for the moon. "Sweetheart, we can't see the moon right now, only its light. It's hidden behind the clouds."

She doesn't mind, she's just happy to be out and about.

"Would you like to go down to the Rose Garden? We can look at the city lights. That's where Daddy proposed to Mommy."

"*Oh God!* Don't remind me!" Jen remarks, triggered by the past, "I can't believe what you've put me through in the last three-and-a-half years."

"Hey, Jen," I say, "we haven't even *known* each other for three years." I add, half jokingly, "I'm sure it *feels* like longer."

We walk down the path of the historic street car line in silence, Jen carrying Sierra, myself hanging back a few paces to let the wave of resentment roll on through.

Once at the overlook, the three of us sit on the historic bench for a moment. But Sierra wants to keep moving. She's been walking now for five months, each day growing more confident.

"Would you like to go down and smell the roses?" Jen asks.

"*Wroses!*" Sierra squeals, vigorously nodding her head.

With Jen on her left and me on her right, we each offer her a finger to wrap her little hands around. With a firm grip on each of us, she leads us down the path and into the garden. From there she guides us across the Hayward Fault, leading us past the upper plots, under the redwood pergola, down through the stepped, concentric plantings to the place where the three forks of Codornices creek emerge as one. There, at the opening, she has us pause and listen to the water. Then, taking us each by the hand again, she leads us back up, the three of us stopping to sample the roses' heavenly scents. In the low light, with the quiet roar of the city rising up from below, the smell is particularly fragrant.

Though neither one of us know it right now, in three weeks Sierra will go to her grandparents and Jen and I will return to the place where we met, Burning Man, and there we will set the intention to let go of the hurt and resentment, allowing it to be swallowed by the stark vastness of the Black Rock desert. In the spirit of allowing the best to come forward, Jen will cease using her first name and start going by her middle name, Epiphany, which is also the name of her mother and her grandmother. We will watch the sun rise all six mornings we are there. The pilgrimage will be a celebration and a time of healing and resetting, and, with matters of the heart, incomplete. But from that place we will begin the hard work of forging a new path, not as individuals, not just as seed DNA for our child, nor as husband and wife, but as partners and friends.

People often ask me how we've managed to turn things around. I don't believe anything is ever turned around completely. Humans are mysteriously complex, relationships even more so. Though the coveted and creative space of love between individuals is universally celebrated, it takes work. As soon as one thing seems resolved, other hurts, both new and old, are free to surface. As each layer is removed, others are exposed and need to be addressed. That being said, we have made remarkable progress. From this perspective, I can begin to identify a few things that have and haven't worked for us.

First, the Buddhist practices I brought into the relationship—including meditation and retreat practices—though serving me as an individual, were actually detrimental to our relationship in the beginning. Why? Because I used them as justifications for my ego-based holy war against Epiphany. Instead of loving or promoting the spiritual growth of the other, I whacked her over the head with my world view. More specifically, based on my own fear of intimacy, I used the Buddhist teachings to condemn Epiphany's desire to spend more time with me. Though I believe in the power and importance of religion, I have certainly been guilty of using it in the worst ways possible.

When we could see that we were beginning to develop bad habits, we started going to couples' counseling. The results were limited. The problem with talk therapy was that both Epiphany and I were damn good at it. I was especially good at twisting things around, getting the therapist on my side (at least when she was no longer around to monitor our exchanges), and using them against Epiphany. Even a summer-long attempt to learn and use Nonviolent Communication techniques proved to be no more than warm-up exercises for screaming matches.

Next was Neurolinguistic Programming (NLP), a practice of using audio, visual, and kinesthetic cues to access the wisdom of the subconscious. NLP has proved to be far more effective for both of us by allowing us to address the hurt behind our frustrations *directly* without continuously rehashing our stories. Our work with NLP, specifically with trainers Tim and Kris Hallbom and with a particularly dedicated NLP coach named Therese Kells, has led to numerous experiential insights for both of us, including the momentum of our family dynamics and the subtleties of our relationship and how it intersects more universal themes unfolding in the human drama. Much of the earlier Ground of Creativity chapter, for example, specifically the section on the dawn of conscious self-awareness, was based on insight gained during a marathon NLP therapy session with Therese.

Next is dancing, specifically to intensely loud, electronic music built on the thick foundations of bone-rattling sub-bass. Wearing ear plugs, we frequently enter into the tempestuous oceans of sound. The engulfing sound and raw energy allow us to let our guards down, roll about for a spell, and reenact our initial meeting. We nearly always emerge with a sense of renewed love and possibility. Since our relationship was born out of music and dancing, we have the good fortune of using these as our go-to singularity of sorts. We've learned to return there often, using them as a reset button.

We have since developed other tricks to get out of our own heads and into our hearts, but I'll save those for another time.

And of course there's Sierra, whose unfettered spirit and perpetual wonder and aliveness have been guiding us both along. When Epiphany and I look at her, we experience the wholeness and mystery of the universe looking back at us, gifting us with the opportunity to care for her and for one another.

After Sierra was born, for example, I'd often sit with her in the rocking chair, studying her tiny features. Some days what struck me was the fragility of this little person, completely dependent upon us. Other days, I sensed something far more enduring, an old and wise spirit that had been around for eons. One day, when the winter light was just right, I noticed two spirals of hair on her head, the first originating from the crown, the other of much finer, almost invisible wisps swirling outwards from her forehead, just above her left eye. When compared to the first, this second spiral seemed to be a sort of follicular anti-matter, a boundary to keep the other spiral from overrunning her entire face. I could also see that this was to become the same force sculpting her maternal grandfather's distinct cowlick, as well as Epiphany's widow's peak. Already, this second spiral has disappeared, leaving, as geologists like to say, a relic landscape.

As products of a dynamic, interdependent, deeply mysterious, wildly creative universe, I have come to think of our own lives progressing like those two spirals, one representing all that we can plainly see, and another, much larger spiral representing all that lies hidden from view. The second spiral, like the Divine Ground of the perennial philosophers, gives form and significance to the first, as well as space in which to grow.

Furthermore, as I've watched this little spirit descend into and occupy her mind and body, I wonder how much of what we do comes from our own efforts, and how much of it is simply the tides of things much bigger rolling through, driven by the more enduring celestial bodies of wisdom, love, and compassion and their opposites, ignorance, hatred, and cruelty.

Neither Epiphany nor I are proud of how we handled ourselves during the pregnancy, nor for that matter in the period soon after Sierra was born. We had, as Buddhists like to say, a lot of karma to ripen together. Like our little girl navigating the birth canal, forward and back, we've both had to work hard rebirthing a new version of ourselves, enduring the pain of regression, ushered on by the levity of growth and deepening connection.

We're inexpressibly grateful that we both stuck it out. To care for a little person who's in a constant state of becoming, whose natural disposition is wonder and amazement, and whose spirit shines unobstructed in the time before identity, has been indescribably precious and healing for us both. A piece of our hearts, now, is out there in the world, leading us along. As we change her diapers and rock her to sleep, as we feed her and clothe her and bathe her at night, as we inhale her vitality and tell her how much we love her, she leads us along toward our own, heretofore impossible, maturations.

All of which is my reason for including this chapter in the book: This whole experience, as painful and overwhelming as it was and as nourishing and empowering as it's become, has also been, by far, my single biggest lesson in creativity to date.

For Epiphany and, despite all our fears and insecurities, all our limiting beliefs and blame, and all our battles in the months before the pregnancy, we chose to enter the game. In the face of our deepest fears, we chose to bring new life into the world, then held on as best we could as the universe kept presenting us with challenge after challenge, each one wrenching us from our own forms of self-centered behavior, challenges to aid us in accepting the situation as it was, challenges, ultimately, to make us more available to the child, and, in time, to each other. The external experience of creativity usually involves putting things together. The internal experience of becoming a creator, however, often involves pulling self-imposed limitations apart.

My profound and irrefutable insight to have the child did not mean that everything was going to align perfectly from that point on. All genuinely creative undertakings are transformative processes. Once we decided to enter into the crucible, some pain was almost guaranteed, because neither one of us was ready. How could we be? Most of us don't move through the world without the momentum of the past affecting the conditions of the present, and the past for both Epiphany and I had been solely to *ourselves*.

In Epiphany's and my case, each of us felt the strong attraction to one another on both a physical and spiritual plane, but our ego identities and all our stories and schemas, all our underlying scripts about how things should or should not be, were running the show. From the moment we woke up from fitful sleep, until the moment we lay down in exasperation, we battled one another for sovereignty, wanting the other to surrender to our own, very limited way of viewing things.

My whole relationship with Epiphany has been an initiation of sorts, converting me from a dyed-in-the-wool individual out for myself to a valued member of the communities with whom I interact. I can honestly say that I've taken my seat in this world and have committed myself to helping others through my design work, through the universal appeal of creativity and the creative process, and through my own budding NLP practice. Not only was Sierra Lucia born from this process, so, too, was this book, forcing me to focus in the face of all my new responsibilities.

And for Epiphany, a true extrovert with a habit of taking on other people's existential projects, she has learned to set up appropriate boundaries, create a sense of greater autonomy, and care less and less about how others perceive her.

I am profoundly grateful that Epiphany, who, with her uncanny ability to see my defense structures from the beginning, took the most important stand of all. "You're the one!" she said, on the second day we were together, which scared the hell out of me. And, even more confounding, as she said later told me, the spirit who would become Sierra, a spirit who had been with her since she was a little girl confirmed it, saying, "*He's the father.*"

Both my wife and my daughter, and the whole of this experience, as challenging as it was and as challenging as it sometimes continues to be, have helped me to step outside the confines of my head and enjoy the expansiveness of my heart, and *to create*, to create new projects, to create new opportunities, to create new life, and to have new chances to delve deeper into this awesome and mysterious world in which we live.

REQUEST TO THE READER

Thank you for taking the time to read *The Shoreline of Wonder: On Being Creative*.

I wrote this book for two main reasons: 1) To satisfy my own desire to better understand creativity and the creative process and 2) to inspire others to experience their own innate creativity and to begin sharing their own unique creative gifts with the world. My long term goal is to bring these ideas, and the practices I'll be developing in my next book, *Further Along the Shoreline of Wonder: How to Live a Creative Life*, into businesses, nonprofit organizations, governmental agencies, school systems, and spiritual congregations, helping individuals and organizations to grow and to thrive by embracing a creative life.

As such, I am dependent upon you, the reader, to know what sort of impact *The Shoreline of Wonder* has had on you. If any part of this book has inspired, confused, motivated, or enraged you, please send your comments and feedback to austin@austinhillshaw.com. Positive and negative alike, I am appreciative for any feedback you're willing to give as it allows me to evaluate what is and isn't working. If your experience in reading this book has been overwhelmingly positive, I would be grateful for any review or testimonial you're willing to write.

Finally, as a student of creativity, I want to know about your own experiences with creativity and the creative process. If you'd like to share your own ineffable experiences of insight, the challenges you faced while manifesting a project, and/or your experiences with Self-expression, please send those, too. Through your willingness to share, I continue to learn, grow, and improve my ability to convey this important information.

Thank you again for your help. As a reminder of what Christo said on interdependence, "Everybody here is part of my work. If they want it or they don't want it, anyway, they are part of my work... they are an integral part of making [this] project."

With great appreciation,

Austin Hill Shaw
Berkeley, California
October 2012

ACKNOWLEDGMENTS

This project has unfolded over eight years, with innumerable experiences of insight, false starts, dead ends, signs of progress, helpful critiques, desire to cast it all aside, and clear messages that I needed to continue. In a dynamic, interdependent, deeply mysterious universe, the work as a whole has been initiated, shaped, put on the back burner, resumed with great verve, plagued by seemingly impossible obstacles, re-engaged, reshaped, refined, and, for now, turned into a completed project. All of these steps forward, backward, and side to side have been influenced by a complex web of interrelatedness, all around the questions: "What is creativity, why is it universally revered, and how best to engage it?"

As such, I am inexpressibly grateful to all the people, teachings, books and essays, films and recordings, conversations, and those unexpected moments of clarity that have led to the words you see before you. Here is but a small but important sampling of those who have made this possible.

To begin, I would like to thank my parents, my mother and father, and my stepparents, Al Feld and Janet Shaw, for your unyielding support and overwhelmingly positive nurturing and influence throughout my life. I have learned something profound from each and every one of you, and, as one who has chosen a less than conventional path, I've felt your love in all its forms, including appreciation, curiosity, enthusiasm, and, at times, valid concern. I also want to thank my newest parents, Jim and Epiphany Long, for your unconditional support for Epiphany and I, and your connection to and nurturing of Sierra Lucia. I also want to express my love for my brothers, Tony, Eric, and Devin, and for my sister, Krista. I love our unique and unusual siblinghood.

I am also indebted to my friendships, first and foremost, to my lifelong friendship with William James Okin. We've know one another before we had the capacity to say each other's names, and our lives have been intertwined ever since. Your brilliant mind, your irreverence, and our long history together have been a source of joy and calibration for over four decades now.

I would also like to thank all those friendships that have been forged over adventure and, by association, long conversations along trails, in campgrounds, and in wild, media-free environments. On the climbing front, I'd like to thank Dr. Eran Hood, my climbing partner on the Rostrum and many other routes, Billy Key and his wife, Deanne Buck, Amy Barnhorst, John Gardner, Eliza Kerr, my friend and guide to the Basque Country, Gorka Martinez, and the late Mathew Baxter. In the surfing realm, I'd like to thank Michael Kang, Morgan Bazilian, Zeb Esselstyn, and our gracious host and king of the notorious Dominical beach break, Brendan Jaffer and his wife, Sofiah Thom. Whether we were laughing hysterically, nearly drowning, or sipping chilled tequila at the end of the day, my time spent with you all has been wonderfully enriching.

Next, I would like to thank the Men's Circle for its honest, purposeful support for almost three years now. My reintegration into the vortex of the Bay Area after a 15-year absence, my initiation in marriage and fatherhood, and my ability to finish this book have been made possible by the sacred container we help create on a weekly basis. Most especially, I'd like to thank Aaron Pava for spearheading its inception, David Shakiban and Tim Aldridge for first bringing it to my awareness, master stone-shaper Mykael David Lazzeri for being my first sponsor, and all my teammates, including Tom Bennigson, Michael Stutz, Leroy Watts, Rob Buchinski, Mathias Zeumer, Ron Masters, Kenny Duncan, Noah Bruce, Steve Sporer, John Roth, Mathew Taylor, Felipe Parker, Yari Mander, Kaleem Zia Khwaja, and Peter Schurman from Ra, and John Van Dinther, David Schlussel, Damian Sol, Matt Green, and Mykael David Lazzeri from Ujjayi, and Tosh Stone, Michael Blacksburg, David Silva, Mark Michael Lewis, Kevin O'Malley, Gary Fernandez, Adam Gyokuzan Coutts, and Jonathan Mandel from the circle at large. Outside The Circle, the mysterious Simon Kang and the king of seduction, Hristiyan Atanasov, have also played pivotal role in my life. Each one of you has been invaluable in my transformation from an individually focused nomad to a powerful, rooted man and leader in my communities.

I'd also like to thank the people who have contributed to my understanding of design, a unique and challenging subset of creativity. They include Kat Vlahos, Keith Loftin, and Michael Jenson from the University of Colorado, Denver, Sergio Palleroni, Steve Badanes, and Jim Adamson from the University of Washington, Javier Cenicacelaya from La Universidad del Pais Vasco, in Donostia/San Sebastian and my employer in Bilbao, and, perhaps most importantly, Mike Moore, cofounder of Tres Birds Workshops, whose abstract model of a human spine and his amazing abilities as a designer and an athlete never cease to amaze me. I'd also like to thank my friends and clients, those who have entrusted me to design their homes and businesses, even when more qualified designers were available. Among those courageous souls I'd like to thank Patrick and Amy Sweeney, Cathy Weisz, Erik Singer, and Dr. Matt Green.

I'd also like to thank those people who have helped me with the craft of writing and the preparation of this book for publication. First I would like to thank my Mom, an avid reader and barometer of my headiness who, at first and rightly so, dreaded receiving most everything I sent her. Sy Safransky, editor of *The Sun*, helped me to understand the significance of writing as a spiritual path during a conversation with him at a 2007 writing retreat at Esalen in Big Sur, California. Ron Takaki, in a kind and grandfatherly way, was instrumental in encouraging me to introduce stories and narratives to the manuscript. My father-in-law, Jim Long, has been more than gracious pouring over earlier chapters well before anything was near completion. Professor Brook Landon's palpable love of writing and his stellar lecture series, *Building Great Sentences: Exploring the Writer's Craft*, gave me the tools and inspiration to build interesting, readable sentences. Following Julia Cameron's suggestion to write three pages every day for 12 weeks without re-reading or editing was worth its weight in gold and produced most of the seeds of the chapters for my forthcoming book, *Further Along the Shoreline of Wonder: How to Live a Creative Life*. My editor and heart sister, Maxima Kahn, has done wonders helping me to make sense of difficult subjects and challenging me over and over to honor the needs of the reader. The inimitable Robert Heger, a true Renaissance man, was the first to read through my manuscript and provide me, most importantly, with the gift of genuine appreciation, even when it was still missing the penultimate chapter and the final edits. Morgan Bazilian gave me strong pointers on how to improve the text. Our amazing nanny to Sierra, Jenn Sartor, whose has become a friend and integral part of our family, compiled the recommended readings section. Elizabeth Whipple, who did extensive edits on *Between the Bridge and the Water: Death, Rebirth, and Creative Awakening*, helped with the final copy proofing. Jonathan Mandel and I had a blast taking headshots at his home in San Francisco, including the one on the back cover. And, in the last month of putting this together, I was incredibly fortunate to be put in touch with graphic designer Katelyn Schirmer and her best friend from high school, book designer Lisa Paul. Wow! I love your aesthetics, enthusiasm, teamwork, and celebration of sensual qualities of books. Thank you for making this beautiful and visually pleasing to read!

Providing access to the umbrella awareness that makes everything possible, I'd also like to express my love for all my teachers. Thank you to Patrick Sweeney for teaching me how to meditate, for introducing me to the lineage of Chögyam Trungpa, and for facilitating the three-month Rainy Season Retreat where the initial insight to write on creativity first took hold. I'd also like to thank Lourdes Alvarez, Kate Baldwin, Andi Tillmann, Forest Perrupato, Diana Villaseñor, David Wiley, and Eliot Cowan for opening my eyes to the living wisdom of the natural world. Thank you to David Ledeboer for his ability to braid the streams of the patriarchal qualities of Vajrayana Buddhism and the matriarchal wisdom of the primal religions and all the healing that has resulted. Special thanks to my neighbor, Zachary Markwith, who finished his book *One God, Many Prophets: the Universal Wisdom of Islam* while I was finishing mine. Our conversations on the porch, and our mutual respect and appreciation for the path blazed by Huston Smith, have created a much needed *sangha* for me.

My environment being an important factor, I'd like to honor the power and beauty of the Golden Gate and my chosen city's orientation to it, Berkeley, California. Although I wrote parts of this book in many places, it was completed here, its powerful orientation in relation to the Golden Gate a contributing factor. I would also like to thank the University of California for use of the Doe Library and the East Asian Library, and the City of Berkeley for the Main Branch of the Berkeley Public Library for providing me with inspiring, well-lit spaces and sturdy, uncluttered desks upon which to write.

I'd like to thank the Sierra Nevada and the Universal Ground of Everything for providing me a place of refuge, reflection, and regeneration. Thank you to the most beautiful mountains I've had the pleasure of animating, Padmasambhava Peak, Vajrayogini, and Dorje Trolö, Karma Pakshi. Thank you, Grandfather Fire and Grandmother Ocean. May I continue to be a servant of your limitless wisdom and compassion as I spiral about, continuing to take my seat in this world.

And finally, I would like to thank my wife, Epiphany, for being a stand for love and for giving me the gift of marriage and fatherhood, and to our daughter, Sierra Lucia, for being unfathomably amazing. I once heard that in an effort to put a man on the moon, the Kennedy Space Program took all of human knowledge up to that point and doubled it. You've both done the same for my heart.

END NOTES BY CHAPTER

Introduction: The Ground and the Path of Creativity

The quote from Mary Oliver came from a recent visit to Yosemite to celebrate the 10-year wedding anniversary of my friends' Eliza and Nate Kerr, while the final edits on this book were underway. There, on a ladder to their daughters' loft, a ladder made by another climbing friend of ours, Lawrence LaBianca, were Mary Oliver's words. Later that afternoon, on the way back to the Bay Area, I stopped to look at The Rostrum and saw a climber standing on the perch where I saw the rainbow.

From The Big Bang, Beginningless Time, and the Journey of the Creative Universe

"Sparklers of emotions" and our tendency to "dominate other species, and castigate outsiders we see as threats" came from Professor Stephen P. Hinshaw's lecture series, *Origins of the Human Mind*, from The Great Courses. After listening to his series over and over, and seeing his photo on the jacket liner, I ran into him near the UC Berkeley campus, introduced myself, and took the opportunity to thank him.

My understanding of the work of Mark Rothko, as well as the life-sustaining aspects of creativity for Van Gogh, were inspired by the BBC series, *Simon Schama's The Power of Art*, originally aired in 2006.

My understanding of the Big Bang, the early universe, and the life-cycle stars came from the lecture series *The Joys of Science*, by Professor Robert M. Hazen, also from The Great Courses.

"...the tiniest of wiggly bits at the far edge of time" and the Taoist view of the origins of the universe came from a talk given by Liu Ming at the Golden Gate School of Feng Shui, and subsequent conversations at his home in Oakland. Thank you to Manu Butterworth for allowing me to attend the lecture in December, 2009.

"Growth happens in the light, transformation in the darkness" was spoken to me by Cobb Mountain's *loco roshi,* John Jennings.

A Buddhist view on the origins of the universe came from *The Universe in a Single Atom: The Convergence of Science and Spirituality,* by His Holiness the Dalai Lama.

Cultivating Insight: Isaac Newton and the Law of Universal Gravitation

Lawrence Ferlinghetti's quote came from a pamphlet, "What is Poetry?" which he handed out at the 2005 Ojai Poetry Festival.

My understanding of the significance of Isaac Newton came primarily from *The Joys of Science,* by Professor Robert M. Hazen, The Great Courses.

The William Kentridge quote came from the PBS series, *Art in the Twenty-First Century,* Season 5 (2009), 1, "Compassion."

The quote from Ran Ortner came from his interview with Ariane Conrad, "Water, Water Everywhere: Ran Ortner's Love Affair with the Sea," from the June 2012 edition of *The Sun.* It was one of the most illuminating interviews I've read on water, creativity, and art.

The five qualities of insight were inspired by the chapter, "Mysticism" from William James's *The Varieties of Religious Experience.*

Julia Cameron's quote from *The Artist Way,* "People frequently believe the creative life is grounded in fantasy. The more difficult truth is that creativity is grounded in reality...," is a powerful reminder that creativity is not a departure from the world but a chance to more fully immerse ourselves in it. I am indebted to Cameron for her spiritual approach to creativity and for her "Morning Pages," which has helped free myself of my habit of belaboring sentences.

The quote from Alexander Pope appeared on Isaac Newton's Wikipedia page, as did Newton's quote, "I do not know what I may appear to the world, but to myself I seem to have been only a boy playing on the sea-shore...," which I found after I'd written the bulk of the chapter and settling upon my title, *The Shoreline of Wonder.*

Manifestation: Christo, Jeanne-Claude, and Running Fence

"The strongest man in the world can't even lift his own leg," came from a conversation with my friend David Ledeboer, who spent several years in a Korean Zen monastery.

The specifics, including the materials list of Running Fence, were obtained from Christo and Jeanne-Claude's website, http://www.christojeanneclaude.net/

Most of the quotes and the back story of Running Fence, including the anecdote about General Motors rejecting the material that would become the fabric for the fence, came from watching and listening to the audio commentary on the 1977 documentary film Running Fence, by Albert and David Maysles and Charlotte Zwerin.

I stumbled upon Rollo May's book, *The Courage to Create*, while working in the North Berkeley branch of the Berkeley Public Library, in the summer of 2011.

"I sided with the majority of the people who felt that if the fence did go up, it would bring so many people into the community that it would change us. Well, it did change us. It ended up bringing people together. For the first time the local farmers and ranchers and hippies were getting together and talking about things, and often we were on the same side." Came from "Good Fences Make Friends," an article by Gayle M.B. Hanson, Insight on the News, 10/07/96

I visited the sole remaining Running Fence pole outside the post office during a trip to Valley Ford in the spring of 2011

Self-Expression: Huston Smith and The World's Religions

John O'Donohue's quote came from the interview "The Unseen Life that Dreams Us: John O'Donohue on the Secret Landscape of Imagination and Spirit," by Diane Covington, which appeared in the April 2007 issue of *The Sun*.

The opening sequence was based on Huston's description of his childhood home, in his autobiography, *Tales of Wonder: Adventures Chasing the Divine*. Huston helped me refine in his living room in North Berkeley on November 11, 2011. We went line by line through the beginning and Huston helped me be accurate. "A town of intentionally winding *lanes*, not streets, they were so narrow if I reached out my hands [I could touch the walls]," he said for example. He also sent me off to make copies of chapters from sequel to his autobiography, the soon to be released, *And*

Live Rejoicing. Most profoundly, on my request, we prayed together at the end of our meeting, which made everything brighter. After our prayer, he said to me, "What began as a chore has ended in exuberance."

"...our flashes of insight into abiding light" comes from the final pages of Huston's book *The World's Religions.* The full quote reads "The human opportunity, the religions tell us, is to transform our flashes of insight into abiding light."

Aldous Huxley's four doctrines of the Perennial Philosophy came from his essay, "The Perennial Philosophy," from *Paths Beyond Ego: The Transpersonal Vision,* edited by Roger Walsh and Frances Vaughan.

Huston's quote on the primal religions appeared in *The World's Religions, page 366.*

The Sufi description of imagination being like an isthmus or barzakh came from a conversation with my scholarly neighbor, Zachary Markwith.

"The larger the island of knowledge, the longer the shoreline of wonder," came from Huston's *Beyond the Post-Modern Mind: The Place of Meaning in a Global Civilization.*

The quote from Lao Tzu comes from the *Tao Te Ching,* as translated by Gia-Fu Feng and Jane English (Vintage Books, A Division of Random House, New York, 1972).

To better understand love, I highly recommend M. Scott Peck's book *The Road Less Traveled.* He also lays out the importance of discipline, religion, and the experience of Self-expression, or what he calls "grace".

The letter from William H. Danforth and Huston's overview of his worldly adventures are found in Huston's book *Tales of Wonder: Adventures Chasing the Divine.*

PUTTING IT ALL TOGETHER: THE LIGHT BOX AT PRANA DEL MAR

Erik Singer's reflections on his experience of developing Prana del Mar were recorded over dinner at Osha's Thai Restaurant in downtown San Francisco in August 2012.

Ran Ortner quoting Thomas Merton also came from the interview "Water, Water Everywhere: Ran Ortner's Love Affair with the Sea," by Ariane Conrad, from the June 2012 edition of *The Sun.*

PULLING IT ALL APART: MOONLIGHT ON THE MOUNTAINS

Izumi Shikibu's quote was translated and presented in a talk by Jane

Hirshfield at the 2003 Ojai Poetry Festival, as part of the series, "Poetry in a Time of Uncertainty".

Though the idea of writing the final chapter had been floating about in my head for months, it was initiated by writing the opening lines, on April 1, 2011 in celebration of the two-year anniversary of discovering Epiphany was pregnant.

My understanding of the origins and significance of the labyrinth came from Grace Cathedral's Canon Pastor, Lauren Artress, and her book, *Walking a Sacred Path: Rediscovering the Labyrinth as a Spiritual Practice*. After a period of great difficulty in her life, she had an insight to bring the sacred form to the church and another, accessible 24hours-a-day, to the outer courtyard.

Those unsettling transmissions from the internet on the miracle of life came from BabyCenter.com

In her spirited fashion, Epiphany Shaw poured over the narrative to ensure that I presented a balanced perspective.

RECOMMENDED READINGS[6]

Abram, David, *The Spell of the Sensuous* (Vintage Books, A Division of Random House, New York, 1996).

Arnheim, Rudolf, *Art and Visual Perception: A Psychology of the Creative Eye* (University of California Press, Berkeley, 1954).

Artress, Lauren, *Walking a Sacred Path: Rediscovering the Labyrinth as a Spiritual Practice* (Penguin Group, New York, 1995, 2006).

Baker, Jeff, *Heard Around the Fire, Teachings of Grandfather Fire* (Sacred Fire Press, 2010).

Batchelor, Stephen, *Verses from the Center: A Buddhist Vision of the Sublime* (The Berkeley Publishing Group, New York, 2000).

Bayles, David & Orland, Ted), *Art & Fear: Observations on the Perils (and Rewards) of Artmaking* (Image Continuum Press, USA, 1993).

[6]For an updated list of books and other media on creativity across art, science, and religion, check out www.austinhillshaw.com/resources

Benedikt, Michael, *For an Architecture of Reality* (Lumen Books, New York, 1987).

Benson, Heidi "Lethal Beauty: Survivor Recalls the Day He Jumped," *SFGate.com,* November 2005.

Blaustein, Mel & Flemming, Anne, "Suicide from the Golden Gate Bridge," *The American Journal of Psychiatry,* October 2009, Vol. 166, No. 10.

Bly, Robert, Hillman, James, & Mead, Michael, *The Rag and Bone Shop of the Heart, A Poetry Anthology* (HarperCollins Publishers, New York, 1992).

Brown, Dr. Brene, from TED Talk, June 2010, Houston, TX? http://www.youtube.com/watch?v=X4Qm9cGRub0

Calvino, Italo, *Invisible Cities* (Harcourt Brace & Company, Florida, 1972).

Cameron, Julia, *The Artist's Way* (Tarcher, New York, 2002).

Chödrön, Pema, *When Things Fall Apart: Heart Advice for Difficult Times* (Shambhala Publications, Inc., Massachusetts, 1997).

"Compassion," *Art in the Twenty-First Century,* PBS, (2009).

Conrad, Ariane, "Water, Water Everywhere: Ran Ortner's Love Affair with the Sea," *The Sun,* June 2012.

Cowan, Eliot, *Plant Spirit Medicine* (Swan Raven & Co., North Carolina, 1995).

Covington, Diane, "The Unseen Life that Dreams Us: John O'Donohue on the Secret Landscape of Imagination and Spirit," *The Sun*, April 2007.

Csikszentmihalyi, Mihaly *Creativity: Flow and the Psychology of Discovery and Invention* (HarperCollins Publishers, New York, 1996).

Doczi, György, *The Power of Limits: Proportional Harmonies in Nature, Art, and Architecture* (Shambhala Publications, Inc., Massachusetts, 1994).

de Botton, Alain, *The Architecture of Happiness* (Pantheon Books, New York, 2006).

Eliade, Mircea), *The Sacred & The Profane: The Nature of Religion* (Harcourt Brace & Company, Florida, 1957).

Gayford, Martin & Wright, Karen (editors), *The Grove Book of Art Writing: Brilliant Words on Art from Pliny the Elder to Damien Hirst* (Viking Press, New York, 1998).

Gladwell, Malcolm, *Outliers: The Story of Success* (Little, Brown and Company, New York, 2008).

Grey, Alex, *The Mission of Art* (Shambhala Publications Inc., Massachusetts, 1998).

Groth-Marnat, Gary & Summers, Roger, "Altered Beliefs, Attitudes, and Behaviors Following Near-death Experiences," *Journal of Humanistic Psychology*, Summer 1998, Vol. 38, No. 3.

Hanson, Gayle M.B, "Good Fences Make Friends," *Insight on the News*, October 1996, Vol. 12, No. 38.

Hazen, Professor Robert M., *The Joys of Science,* The Great Courses, Lecture Series.

Hinshaw, Professor Stephen P., *Origins of the Human Mind,* The Great Courses, Lecture Series.

His Holiness the Dalai Lama, *The Universe in a Single Atom: The Converge of Science and Spirituality* (Three Rivers Press, New York, 2006).

Horgan, John, *Rational Mysticism: Dispatches from the Border Between Science and Spirituality.* (Houghton Mifflin Company, New York, 2003).

Huxley, Aldous, *The Perennial Philosophy* (HarperCollins Publishers Inc., New York, 1944).

James, William, *The Varieties of Religious Experience* (Touchtone, New York, 1997).

Joiner, Thomas E., *Why People Die By Suicide* (Harvard University Press, Boston, 2005).

Jung, Carl G., *Man and His Symbols* (Dell Publishing, New York, 1964).

Keen, Sam, *Fire in the Belly: On Being a Man* (Bantam Press, New York, 1991).

Lattin, Don, *The Harvard Psychedelic Club: How Timothy Leary, Ram Dass, Huston Smith, and Andrew Weil Killed the Fifties and Ushered in a New Age for America* (HarperCollins Publishers, New York, 2010).

Lehrer, Jonah, *Imagine: How Creativity Works* (Houghton Mifflin Harcourt Publishing Company, New York, 2012).

Livio, Mario *The Golden Ratio* (Broadway Books, New York, 2002).

Matthiessen, Peter, *The Snow Leopard* (Penguin Group, New York, 1978).

Maysles, Albert & David and Zwerin, Charlotte *"Running Fence,"* (Maysles Films, New York, 1977).

Miller, Henry, *Tropic of Cancer* (Grove Press, New York, 1961.)

Moody, Raymond *Life After Life* (Bantam Press, New York, 1975).

Peck, M. Scott, M.D. *The Road Less Traveled* (Simon & Schuster, Inc., New York, 1978).

Pinchbeck, Daniel, *The Return of Quetzalcoatl* (Penguin Group, New York, 2006, 2012).

Pirsig, Robert M., *Zen and the Art of Motorcycle Maintenance* (Bantam Press, New York, 1974).

Pope, Alexander, Isaac Newtown's Wikipedia page

http://en.m.wikipedia.org/wiki/Isaac_Newton

Rappaport, Roy A., *Ritual and Religion in the Making of Humanity* (Cambridge University Press, Cambridge, 1999).

Ray, Reginald A.), *Indestructible Truth: The Living Spirituality of Tibetan Buddhism* (Shambhala Publications, Inc., Massachusetts,

2000).

Richo, David, *Shadow Dance: Liberating the Power and Creativity of Your Dark Side* (Shambhala Publications, Inc., Massachusetts, 1990).

Roberts, Glenn & Owen, John, "The Near-death Experience" (*British Journal of Psychiatry 1998*).

Rosen, David H., "Suicide Survivors: A Follow-up Study of Persons Who Survived Jumping from the Golden Gate and San Francisco-Oakland Bay Bridges" (*The Western Journal of Medicine*, April, 1975).

Sanford, John A., *The Invisible Partners: How the Male and Female in Each of Us Affects Our Relationships* (Paulist Press, New Jersey, 1980).

Schwartz, Tony, *What Really Matters: Searching for Wisdom in America* (Bantam Books, New York, 1995).

Simon Schama's The Power of Art, BBC Two, October/November (2006), Television.

Smith, Huston, *Beyond the Post-Modern Mind: The Place of Meaning in a Global Civilization* (Quest Books, Theosophical Publishing House, Wheaton, Illinois, 1982).

Smith, Huston, *Tales of Wonder: Adventures Chasing the Divine : An Autobiography*, (HarperCollins Publishers, New York, 2009).

Smith, Huston, *The World's Religions* (HarperCollins Publishers, New York, 1961).

Smith, Huston, *Why Religion Matters: The Fate of the Human Spirit in an Age of Disbelief,* (HarperCollins Publishers, New York, 2001).

Suzuki, Shunryu, *Zen Mind, Beginner's Mind: Informal Talks on Zen Meditation and Practice,* (Weatherhill, Inc., New York, 1970).

Tendzin, Osel, *Like Water Poured Into Water* (Satdharma Press, California, 2006).

Trungpa, Chögyam, *Crazy Wisdom* (Shambhala Publications, Inc., Massachusetts, 1991).

Tsu, Lao, *Tao Te Ching,* Translation by: Gia-Fu Feng and Jane English, (Vintage Books, A Division of Random House, New York, 1972).

Wilbur, Ken, *Integral Psychology: Consciousness, Spirit, Psychology, Therapy,* (Shambhala Publications, Inc., Massachusetts, 2000).

Wilbur, Ken, *A Brief History of Everything* (Shambhala Publications, Inc., Massachusetts, 2006).

Websites

American Foundation for Suicide Prevention
http://www.afsp.org

The American Journal of Psychiatry
http://ajp.psychiatryonline.org/

Christo and Jeanne-Claude
http://www.christojeanneclaude.net/

Professor Thomas E. Joiner, Florida State University
http://www.fsu.edu/profiles/joiner/

Suicide.org
http://suicide.org/suicide-faqa.html

World Health Organization
http://www.who.int/mental_health/prevention/suicideprevent/en/

ABOUT THE AUTHOR

For as long as he can remember, San Francisco Bay Area-based Austin Hill Shaw has been enraptured by creativity and the creative process. Prompted by a life-changing insight gained during a three-month meditation retreat in 2004, he began to explore the subject of creativity in earnest, wanting to understand the opportunities and challenges behind creativity's seemingly universal appeal. Since then, he has amassed a wealth of knowledge regarding creative expression in art, science, and religion, in childhood development and adult maturation, in business and the economy, in product innovation, in intimate and organizational relationships, and in non-ordinary states of consciousness, delving into the very core of what is means to be human. More importantly, he has striven to embody all that he's learned, using his own life as an ongoing experiment, testing and refining his methods in his pursuits as a writer and architectural designer.

In a time of rampant job automation and outsourcing, Austin's message regarding the importance of creativity and how to activate it is swiftly making its way out into the world. Drawing upon an innovative mix of cutting-edge science, artistic expression, and age-old spiritual wisdom, Austin presents a timely and enlivening understanding of creativity, one that ignites the full-person creative potential of individuals and organizations alike. He just released his provocative first book in his *Awakening Creativity Series*, entitled *Between the Bridge and the Water: Death, Rebirth, and Creative Awakening*, and will   release his next book, *Further Along The Shoreline of Wonder: How to Live a Creative Life*, in summer 2013.

Whether he is addressing a large audience or working with an individual, Austin combines visionary insight with heartfelt empathy, profound ideas with unexpected humor, and sobering seriousness with joyful irreverence, all with a remarkable sense of presence. He is a gifted storyteller, with the ability to unpack the complex subtleties of the creative process and present them in a way that can be put to use *immediately*. Through his keynote presentations, writing, personal coaching, and his work with his architecture clients, Austin Hill Shaw is dedicated to helping others awaken their natural creative capacities and to share their creative gifts with others.

Find out more about Austin, his speaking and coaching offerings, and his other creative pursuits at www.austinhillshaw.com